BRIGADE

Indian Army

RAMESH SANGLE

BLUEROSE PUBLISHERS
India | U. K.

Copyright © Ramesh Sangle 2024

All rights reserved by author. No part of this publication may be reproduced, stored in a retrieval system or transmitted in any form or by any means, electronic, mechanical, photocopying, recording or otherwise, without the prior permission of the author. Although every precaution has been taken to verify the accuracy of the information contained herein, the publisher assume no responsibility for any errors or omissions. No liability is assumed for damages that may result from the use of information contained within.

BlueRose Publishers takes no responsibility for any damages, losses, or liabilities that may arise from the use or misuse of the information, products, or services provided in this publication.

For permissions requests or inquiries regarding this publication, please contact:

BLUEROSE PUBLISHERS
www. BlueRoseONE. com
info@bluerosepublishers. com
+91 8882 898 898
+4407342408967

ISBN: 978-93-5989-339-6

Cover design: Tahira
Typesetting: Tanya Raj Upadhyay

First Edition: February 2024

BRIGADE

The wonderful day raised from the hill top, breathing of every moment spun around the cool air, yet fragrances carried by mild wave from east. Activities were seen everywhere without any efforts as easy as ice flux flowing as cotton flying over green fields of its own. Sentry was on his job as usual from one end of the large water string. The water source flowing through those large and small whitish splint and brown protrudes giving a look of shallow bottom down below... Spurred milky water sound was the regular site at most of the places where sentry was making his vigilance from its beginning till the temporary bridges for easy access for those dweller. That was the border of two countries, India and Pakistan. Unseal borders were open to all and early morning exchanges were the regular affair on human ground as both were dependant on each other since long and beginning, but for limited morning hours. Many of them were also watch full for the site like an aged one sitting out of their houses for hours and the river had many stories to share each other's, across the border. Many overseas visitors had such wonderful site to see an example of Indian culture of unique line of control.

Milky water disappeared with the early long sun set rays over the fields around. The sentry stop his walk by the incident, while a young girl was on her run like a poor young dear, but on the other side of river. He kept gauzing her till she went out of the site but his virtue was set, she crossed the border using single wooden log led across by nearby villager. His attention will-o-wisp soon on the shadowed on the slippery marshy river surface. That was the shadow of young boy who was on chase for someone like a tiger holding small fishing net in one hand. Sentry found the boy too went till the bridge but turned back without crossing it. The sentry thought logically about the girl in Ghaghara whereas boy in Lenga-curta, ran after her for something or an affair between them? The boy *across* the river, came nearer where sentry was standing but hardly could make him out his face from such distance, yet kept his eyes on him till he entered in the small house near the stream. Sentry to follow him without his notice till his dwellings went behind the tree trunk but did not get much information but informed to his reliever about the incident. Though at the beginning, sentry was in relief, yet gone restless while on his return. Instead going to his barrack went to his Captain to narrate the free movement of such people near the across the border. He explained how the young boy who was chasing the young girl for the unknown reason for him. Sentry by name Sinha the youngest in the platoon was afraid to speak out at such silent midnight hours when entire troop was at rest. Captains block was quite far from their post who himself shifted and started living in the tents built up for emergency. He went near to his tent and tried to listen whether anyone around him, walked down further to enter, hold himself at the flapped door, found him with his briskly guard standing near to get some instructions at that night. Smart Captain asked guard to bring the waiting person inside the tent. Captain did not allowed the soldier to move out but asked to be there outside till he finished his discussion. Briskly person asked the soldier to get in while the other left hurriedly. Captain was in his casual dress, pulled the bottle of red rum, and poured some quantity from it, looked at the sentry who was in his uniform saluted Captain who changed his chair and asked him too seat by his side, understood something there he would spell out at such odd that too after his duty hours.

Captain, tried to offer him drink that refused to have it but found unable to convince himself. Once again Captain asked him for it to share but still refused. "Dear, friend you are refusing to join with me. But now I order to share part of it" Sentry had no choice to escape but to accept. He wanted to speak something but did not allow till he finishes the red rum. Time passed like flyers but never permitted to speak. Within minute the same briskly arrived with some more drink was unusual for the solider. Captain asked the soldier, "Are you in hurry?" He had no answer but stood up instead continue sitting there. Soldier had many rounds of questions in his head, did not uttered a word till Captain gave a nod for him to speak. Captain asked the Guard "Was that right? "Yes Captain, you were right. "

"Now, Sin haji tell me what information you brought for me?"

Soldier promptly replied, "Sir, I saw the unknown boy who was in kurta pyjama and was chasing one girl but vanished from the seen. I think that girl crossed the river at our side though was stuck by her knee long at some thorny bush. "

"You were right but for such small matter you took such a long time to inform me. That was the matter to locate the unknown boy immediately but instead you were lingering at the flapper?"

"But sir, I could not dare to enter when you both were discussing something. "

"Shame on you Sinhala! Are you waiting for something till the man was dead. Pity on you. In fact you are such a strong soldier and behaving like common man in civil society. Our brigade has a name for smart decision and the action. Anyway in future mind well the military norms. I was fully aware what was happened on the river side but was waiting whether you were aware of it who was at the location or merely standing like a grouted pole?"

"I would follow your instructions, sir. "

"Do not just follow but use brain too!" "And tomorrow someone from our side will accompany you in civilian dress. " His code is sheep. " Continued the Captain.

The other day in early morning soldier began to walk to his post, saw the one complete platoon was marching till the river end and turned back by the same route from where they were noticed and shortly dispersed too in different direction.

The soldier who was earlier casual about the entire episode stared everywhere with his opened eyes expecting any previous mischief might have re appeared. Unknown person was already standing in same location in civil uniform, confirmed the code, and went behind the tree trunk covered by willows at bottom. Soldier shown the place where the young man went inside the brick house having front and back door as well. Soldier also pointed out the place of crossing the land where the stream source starts just below the cliff. The fellow was surfacing the entire area while soldier shown the young man coming out of the house, who was carefree while walking down the rough street parallel to stream. The fellow in civil code removed his binocular and snapped his number of photos within fraction of moment. Soldier saw his smart and quick actions and handed over his camera to soldier. Before the man disappear he followed but hardly crossed him. The civilian fellow crossing before the river purchased the basket half filled by specific kind of fishes. The job by military man was the task but in civilian code to survey the area. He reached the spot from where the young one came out. Area was surrounded by public market mainly for fisheries business. He too was carrying the basket, reached at the door, with intention to see how many were residing inside, looking at those many articles scattered here and there. He saw the mezzanine floor connected by wooden steps temporary fitted and a long rope hanging by the side of it was suggesting many of their adventurous attitude. He had no longer had doubt about the loaded floor with many articles and metallic trunks, likely full of ammunitions. All of sudden he noticed someone who was entering from back door, but the civilian smartly dropped some fishes near door, bent over to collect them. Country man while entering looked at him haughtily but short in curious when found him collecting the muddy fishes from the floor. Civilian went back side of the house to note any other things lying around but found only junk of small boats. He hurriedly sold out those fishes, yet got more than enough money than his expectation. Before crossing the rout that closed down, attempted to cross over and went to soldier who became close to him being silent man. They both together hung around but during having food together, soldier asked the civilian, "Why you did not chase that young boy who had worn coarsely dressed for landing in our country?"

"You were right but to inform you, our troops were already on that job. By this time he would have been caught, if not, would have left in the thickest. "

"Do you feel the platoon was just marching? No they were already dispersed only to show the civilians but they went out in various formation in unexpected direction "

Evidences were teaching him lot about the Brigade and power within their spirit. He saw some of the people across were to lower down the small boat in water that too in shallow water. He thought to use the water route for the voyages, since tress passing hours were over. They were testing the boat for repairs as two were busy in checking for water leakages and shifted to shore once the work was over. In night vigilance dimly found something was moving over water in that dark hours of night but noticed as if lighted cigarette was moving along with the shore. Sometimes the light was slowed down and even stopped moving.

The episode was being narrated by the vigilance when the soldier was present in Captain's tent. By that time the soldier was not afraid of Captain but was more freed by himself, made Captain to ask him. "Now tell me Mr. Sinha, could you tell me the sequence wise what could be intention on the shore side?"

Soldier paused for some time, tried to explain the situation there. He accessed, "since the boat was repaired in morning and was tested in shallow waters and again in dark hours of night they thought the right time to get into their job. The light of cigarette was for their fellow men who might have waited for long hours and to get the indication from their fellow men on the way to load something unknown to us."

"Smart enough" said the Captain. Continue further, " Let us understand they were the same people in morning hours who repaired the boat and sailed them through the stream. Now tell me where we are concerned and affected by our position to mislead us. They might be fishermen on the job, reaching at their destination at the cliff where water take turn and some part flows to the large lake nearby?"

Soldier tried to grasp the situation and visualised, "Possible sir, but their intention might be to start the fishing early in morning before someone make bigger catch. They would reach there earlier than other for that intending to stall the boat at early rise of morning rays."

Captain reached near to him holding his glass of rum and the bottle in another hand. Soldier got afraid, went a step back, but he was asked to hold the glass, had no other option but to obey the order out of fear. Captain smiled and pat him, was sensed his logic as was on the right path. Soldier retrieved Captain's faith back.

Captain felt very happy with his answer and decided to give him change over on less speculative work than the absolute one. Border gone busy than earlier days. But soldier was yet was not happy regarding the unfinished task about the girl who fled from the place and crossed in to Indian soil. News of the unknown man with his coarse attire failed in his attempt but was trapped. Before could manage to slip into forest was another cause to be added but could not open the topic as Captain was fully aware of the entire situation like a meteoric on our soil for the day.

Captain could read his face to open up his mind but he did not. Soon he talked to him to send him to join the intelligent group of scot who himself refused the suggestion before issuing the order. The soldier asked him to retain at the defence where he was most needed and his involvement in direct fight with enemy at rigorous, any site.

Captain said, "Dear, I need you in my regiment. You are pride of our brigade. "

Soldier surprised at those words. Information so far passed by him, proved valuable. Some part of border at the other end was engaged with multiple moment of troops with ammunitions. Site was looking like an undeclared war. Information received was being part of regular exercise. Captain and other were fully aware of their motive but did not want to alert the enemy.

By that time Captain send him for training and then immediately was sent for actual war rehearsal where they all have to survive themselves in every odd situation and also live without food for some time. They themselves had to find the water sources to trench the thrust. Soldier found it definitely tough being new to the cadre, gone almost half by his body weight also felt week. He was left alone in the thickest and thorny places where it was not less than any life punishment but could succeeded the test, came out of the dark thickest, fully torn clothing, grown up bear and curled hair on his head. Face was beyond recognition, charred by sunrays and the bush fire he passed through. Captain reached the spot to recognise him too had to get close. Only eyes were to speak about themselves whose wet eyes confirmed that the same one was got through the real test he passed. He was not only patted but immediately took along with him to the nearest hospital for treatment. Soldier suffered more than others being youngest and less experienced who was put for hard test because of his confidence and proved fit for the future defence in order.

War was already in progress, but at the other end of Indian Soil where Captains battalion had no chance to get into it but to be alert. Soldier being under treatment wanted to re-join with those troops fighting on border and were engaged in war activities. By that time many of them returned and joined once again with the company across the border at west front. On observing such incidents, one of the soldier though was seriously injured, wished and spoke to Hospital in charge to get him somehow relieved. He became restless and spoke, indenting to break the rules of the hospital. Doctor who was in charge got alerted himself, put additional guard to prevent him if any such move he chose to do so. Shift doctor under pretext of medicine gave him little more dose of sleeping tablets in his saline. The Solider was very alert but could not help himself. His awareness was so much lively to get every information through newspaper and radio. And even newly admitted injured one. Ward boys and nurses were also were trying to be away from him, as would affect other patient on discussion. Doctor finally shifted him where the wars details were displayed to keep him quite on his bed. He too enjoyed the troops forwarding near Karachi and some another places. War was over! More and more injured were admitted on additional beds even on floor. Winning and Indian flag hoisting was seen beyond the border and cheer for troops everywhere was clear on Television screen, could not hold himself, shouted in joy. Off course even hospital staff too gathered near the scene for the movement. The soldier was moving around and trying to help those incoming injured one and asking everyone nearby for their immediate need when others were busy for the similar help

War was won by Indian Army and acquired most of the border site and interior cities. Though the war was called off but tragic life of those injured were never recovered back or even loss of life. Russians decided to intervene between Pakistan and India being close friends since beginning of free India. Meeting between Indian prime minister, Shri Lal Bahadur Shastra and then Pakistani Prime Minister – Mohammad Ayub Khan was arranged in Tashkent, in Russia. ———. Then Indian Defence Minister Shri. Yeshawantrao Chavan was along with him for his him, though Shri Shastri himself was great statesman. All those defence personnel were curious to hear the result and were in control of the conquered land. That was unusual experience and feel of the time as conquest! Every individual had feel of conqueror of conquest land. Within few days it was learnt that negotiation was appeared for returning of conquest land and consequently news of the death of Indian Prime Minister. Shock wave across the country was so much that, every one forgotten the settlement that occurred because of simultaneous death taken place in other country, pave the way to think of some foul. Many conclusion melted down as time passed but the Defence people never forgotten the defeat in settlement that took place that too when our defence minister was along with him. What could have really happened could not be judged but never forgotten. The soldier as individual never forgot slogan he had given to country –Jay Jawan – Jay Kisan. . . Shasrijee, s slogan was never forgotten by entire defence people, being most of them were from farmer's family, sacrificing their life for the country. All were real son of the land in every respect that made them still stronger than earlier and were prepare even for next adventure that too was expected in near future. The only defeat was in 1962 by China, proved be back a stabber. This political defeat was because of Indian then Prime Minister Pundit Jawaharlal Nehru. Who believed China's Prime Minister Chua end lay? His trust on Panch-sheel was like ten commandment, was a foul and killed our many soldier in the eastern Himalaya, in sea chin sector. We lost the territory, most of the part of sea chin from where the half of the china could be visualised and watched. Then defence minister Menon had to resign because of his negligence to update and make every effort to protect India and Indian land. That political failure and not issuing the order to fire to those who were protecting the land on the border, without any preparation. They had old rifle, machine and stein guns. Their deterred mind courage could fight with enemy without any protective attire which was the need of the hour. Pretty old uniform, torn out woollen socks and shoes did not prevented them but survival in odd chilly condition, temperature below 34 celsisius was another challenge they mate and shown to chine's army how one India is stronger than hundred Chinese soldier.

Indian defeat on both front was taken seriously when first Indian Prime Minister Pundit Jawaharlal was dead. His death was because of brain hammer age. Entire Indian defence was redesigned by Indian new Prime Minister Lal Bahadur Shashri. Yeshwantrao Chavan who was Chief of Bombay State of Maharashtra and Gujarat, was appointed as Defence Minister after the first ever defeat after freedom. Entire Army was updated by him through modern technology and alerted to be ready for any situation or attack by enemy. Every day appeared like a new beginning for Indian Army. Earlier Defence minister had to face rough days in Indian parliament, even after his resignation.

Those who wounded, almost recovered from their physical state, wanted to learn new methods and high tech instruments to know the every movement of enemy in future.

After signing the Tashkent agreement, all tents and temporary measures were taken away from the border site. Many of them returned to their own barracks. Even Captain returned to his head quarter. The solider was busy in learning something new technique was called by Captain. He reported to him was thinking to talk about instrumental technique he had in his mind. Before he could put forward his intention, he was shown some photos of the site where a group of many soldier from many countries together were marching to the site like Lebanon. The group was Peace keeping force working in between two nations to keep them away from war.

Soldier asked Captain who was now recently promoted as Major and appointed to train the troop in the Brigade, "Sir, may I know the reason of showing all these photos? "

Major asked him to seat in front of him to make him comfortable. He said to him in quite soft way. "Listen Sinha. We are proud of you. You succeeded the task that we gave. Now you have to go for another venture but out of country. Our commander in chief promoted for the higher position with a star. You will be going to Cambodia ~~~ as the company head where many other countries would join to participant. At least 30 Indian soldier would be under you initially and you may have to lead many more from other countries too!"

Soldier was surprised at his words which was seconded by Major. He himself was not sure at such words as never participated in actual war or even any war type venture itself. He himself felt more conscious, even for his promotion that too with the two stars on his shoulder. He was worried whether is he fit for the rank he was offered? The Major understood his feelings, clarified, "Mr. Sinha, you did not know the way you worked on the border. Your even casual attempt to note the movement of the boy who was running after the girl and next day his night activities and slipping to Indian soil was the sign of spying for war activities were confirmed by expert. That was how the next day scot was marching near the place where you were centring. Quietly and quickly everything was organised. Our head quarter noted your sharpness and systematic reporting to me. Our secret services were smart enough and supported by our newly appointed honourable defence minister.

The soldier was happy at those confidence shown at him, continued his further quarry, asked, " Sir, thank you for all that, but how many days I will be there ? Because I feel being out of the country, I would be missing any future venture or war. I am sure our enemy might not seat quite but would find out the reason for next attempt at the other end of border. "

"Yes! That would sure to happen but that should not be chance you out from your future progress too! " Major advised him

"I am not a man of that nature where country is the first priority. "

"Good enough! By going out of country and learning many other adventure would rather help in many ways than what you have experienced so far. "

Finally Sinha decided to take his advice

Major immediately replied, "I am happy myself, the way I could convince you. Let me tell you even enough war preparation will not help if never approved politically for action. We lost China war only on such ground. Our soldiers were dying on border while having rife in hand, fingers on trigger but could not fire a single round being not received the order, resulted in loss of thousands of leaves. Tragic end of war because of politicians will and power they possess. When you will be with other countries troops, you may face this kind of attitude and time to time changes in order"

Major could read his face who was carefully listening the norms of defence and thought of himself, looked sharply over and called out if that was himself.

Major continued, said. "Let us go to library. I will show you a film where U. N. forces were deployed. " Major took out some reel of film to display him on projector.

"Be seated officer in this chair and observe every man and soldiers around. Civilians are moving freely in market area but no one knows when and what could happen. Now you could judge the country is from western side. Bitter cold could be seen from those people having worn woollen coats and jacket. You can see behind the market those high hills covered by toll pine trees and some water stream leaping to east end where collective water mixed to the large pond but other side of hill. That was the major area where terrorist take safe place to hide or cross the lake if chased by the force. Now you can see the immediate incident that had taken place. "

All of sudden a group of people, masked face, descended down from the hilly area, opened fire on the moving mob in crowded market area, injuring many of them and slipped into pine forest. Military personal followed, but returned empty handed. That was regular affair in spite of U. N. Resolution who had number of meetings with those separatist, yet some of them were never under their control.

Major exhibited number of such incidents where war like situation raised, but wait and watch situation was more dangerous than war. Here the world experts work out some solution and we were being the peace keeping force had to follow their decision. Here we did not had any say! Sinha pretended not having satisfied with that situation but the major was sure about his interest, said "Now I will show another filmed situation. "

That was island far at south-eastern coast. Morning hours looked pretty cool though the breeze was stopped. Island was covered by silvery sand, looked like carpet on plains. At the end of those edges was thick forest, quite heighted trees, where those many clouds of birds were the flying over. When everything was calm on beach, sun was bright and hot at noon. Sea was silent like the water in pond. At the relaxed hours of evening, small boat at the horizon appeared. Birds from east appeared in groups flying towards the west side woods. Many of them already arrived and sat on those trees. Before getting dark the boat turned near those heavy rocky area. Some youngsters in group of 7-8 were seen coming from other end of beach, had some bottles in hand was the sign heavily drunk, were intermittently getting scattered. The boat had turned its direction, was still in water trying to understand where those youngsters were trying to reach. Soon they launched the boat at some distance, jumped in the water, rifle and guns in hand, shoot out more than 5-6 boys, but two of them managed to slip from the site. Boat again turned to the rocky place where possible of their destination or regular storing place of those terrorist. Within hour the pare troop arrived saw the boat was being launched. Next day large force arrived well equipped, to the spot at that rocky place but did not get anything except some clothes and kitchen ware. While on wait, after some time they heard some scream and its echo, together with group of birds flying thither whither. Suddenly all soldiers rose and rushed in the direction of sound and those flying birds. Though the kind of anticipation of terrorist was possible, but in that thickest anything was possible. When they went near and found nothing, but cry of anger of the tribe couple who were collecting dry streak for winter.

Film was over. Sinha was quite for some time. In both incident military was like a check over terrorist without any result. Major could read him, said, "The group of terrorist were fled unpunished. That was possible only when some information in advance was received from those dwellers around or even elsewhere. Only their togetherness and will full unique attitude would work then only our aim of being fulfilled. "

All this time he was feeling stuff. He felt and feeling could be seen on his face. Major came forward, holding his wrist, said, "I know, by this time you might have gone bored at my repeated advices. But the brigade is expecting lot from you. " As he finished, patted him on his shoulder, made Sinha happy, made his mind in a moment and inspired to accept the order.

Soon after getting confidence within him, Major reminded him as precaution, " Look Sinha, you have to be always alert while on island. You have to keep your eyes open for those who are regular seafaring and casual hunters. Also while in town, should understand those regular dwellers and strangers. You should make out that inhabitant from casual visitors. For that you have to peer round the corner like a spy.

At the time of signing the letter, he asked administrator in presence of Major, "How many years this assignment will last?"

"It would last for three to five years. "

He immediately thought to revamp his project, asked Major and administrator to allow him to be here in this compass for few days so that he could go through those books on U. N. resolution. After getting required information he would leave for his village for a month on pre village leave and there after resume his duties.

That was agreed and right from the day he was regular visitor to library for a week. He was sitting late night and writing all the information needed for his projected work. It seems he had some overseas plan while on his job. He could get those books on shelf, found little dusty being not handled by anyone of readers.

Name of book was — The Indian Peace Keeping Force at U. N.

————————he had written all he wanted as follow.

So far India has taken part in 49 peace keeping mission—contributing exceeding 1, 80, 000 troops and significant number of police personal having around world.

In many missions, protection of civilians and support peace process to bring the situation under control. In Eritrea, Indian Engineers helped to rehabilitee roads as part of the U. N. Mission in Ethiopia and Eritrea.

In many missions protection of civilians is the heart of our mandate. Blue Hamlets are protective population against threat and contributing to a secure the representation of final military in U. N. peacekeeping operation.

We work alongside U. N. Police and civilian colleagues to promote stability, security and United

Nations military personal are the Blue Hamlets on the ground. Troop must know what to do if they find themselves in an ambush, for example—

1— U. N. Peace keeping force helps countries navigate the difficult path from conflict to peace.

2—It is led by department of peace operation of U. N.

3— U. N. peacekeepers provide security and political and peace building support to help countries make the difficult, early transition from conflict to peace.

—There are 13 U. N. peacekeeping operations deployed on three continents.

—U. N. peacekeepers (often referred as Blue Berets or Blue Helmets because of their light blue berets or blue helmets has) can include soldiers, police officers and civilian personal.

Peacekeeping monitors and observe peace processes in past conflict area and assist ex-combination in implementing peace agreements.

— Peacekeepers remain members of their respective armed forces and do not constitute an independent "U. N. Army", as U. N. does not have such a force. . .

—Such assistance comes in many forms, including confidence building measures, power sharing arrangement, electro support, strengthening the rule of law and economic and social development.

Principle of U. N. Peace keeping.

UN Peacekeeping is guided by three basic principles.

~ Consent of the parties,

~~Impartiality,

~~Non-use of forces except in self-defence and defence of mandate.

Indian peace keeping have recognised for the strong contribution to building peace in conflict affected South Sudan as well as going alone and beyond their duties to support local communities.

Financing—

The financial resources of UN peacekeeping operation are the collective responsibilities of UN Managers. ~~According to UN. Charter, every member of the state is legally obliged to pay their respective share for peacekeeping.

- Decisions about establishment, maintenance or expansion of peacekeeping operations are taken by the Security Council.
- ~ Role of UNSC in peacekeeping.
- It is Security Council to determine when and where as UN Peace operation should be deployed.
- The Security Council responds to crises around the world on a case-by-case basis and it has a range of option for disposal. It takes many different factors into account

considering the establishment of new peace operation including

- ~~~ Whether there is ceasefire in a place and parties have committed themselves to a peace process indented to reach a political settlement.
- ~~~Whether a cleared political goal exists and whether it can be reflected to the mandate, whether precise mandate for a UN operation can be formulated.
- ~ Whether the safety and security of the UN personal can be reasonably ensured, including in particular whether reasonable guarantees can be obtained from the main parties reflections regarding safety and security of UN personal.

India and UN peace keeping force.

India today is the largest contributor of troops of UN. PEACEKEEPERS.

~~~ More than 200, 000 Indian troops have served in 49 of the 71 UNPKO deployed so far.

~~~ Current mission of India are, ~

~A—Lebanon (UNIFIL) since December

~B—Congo (MONUSG) since January2005

~C~ Sudan South (UNMIS/ UNMISS) since April 2005

~D~Golden Heights (UNDOF) since 2006d

~E—Ivory Coast (UNOCI) since April 2004

~F – Halti (MINUSTTAH) since December 1997.

Many long nights spending at library was never felt tiring but created more acquainted with the place and at the table he sat. That was his last day at the place where he developed and addicted reading more about India Army, their different strategies, latest technology and all that. His time was over at those barracks and had to leave the place with casual send-off that was arranged by Major.

He boarded the train for his village, but instead getting down at his station near to his home town, proceed further and also changed his root leading to India border. He got down at the station where Army was on its return journey. He could not stand with the site. At one end cease fire and negotiation at top level and other end army personnel were being treated on the Railway platform. Entire platform was full of injured soldiers. Most of the areas were covered by clotted blood or fresh droplets on floor while carrying those wounded at every arrived soldiers. Site was in silence and busy with all doctors from military and even from elsewhere and those villagers to support and carry them and dead one on their shoulder, expecting to recover from interments and slow heart beats.

Soldier could not stood with the site rushed to the place and crossed the border. He saw another troop in the same way as earlier where wounded were being carried out on stretcher. He entered quite inside may be few mile where he was halted by some India sentry who was monitoring the operation and checking if anyone is left over. He too was ordering and panicky giving instructions so that no unturned incident could happen. While returning many volunteers and soldier were again and again looking behind where many Indians gave their life and now leaving the land that they conquered. Sinha too could understand their feelings. Today they were conqueror of the land

But leaving it behind as orphan child. Sinha instead turning back straight went ahead. That matter was serious and that too when he gone through the documents of UNISCO. Some soldier from enemy side tried to stop him at gun point but never dithered went ahead snatching his gun. He was at that point and was to shoot him, but reminded himself to be in control. He went further ahead where he found some group of people, might be from nearby villages were gathered together. Though he was unsure about any mishap that would take place any time in the evening. That evening was full of fogy atmosphere and things were unclear near that village nearby. He could see one of the Indian soldiers was profusely wounded and no one was nearby to save him. All those villagers helped to take him near the border where Indian Military camp was situated but with help of Sinha.

Sinha did not stop there but went back to know whether anything is yet to recover. While on run he could get some moment near the bush, slowed himself, walked down to bush found one lame military person was trying to save himself from something, tried to run from the place, leaving his rifle and ammunitions he was carrying. He did followed, but allowed to go him alone. He collected those weapons and ammunitions laying there or left over.

Entire area was took over in silences, except some barking events from the village situated near by forest. He turned back in those quiet and dark hours of late evening. While returning he was mistaken the path through which he appeared here, stood for a while tried to pears his eyes through the intermittent fogy clouds. He followed in a particular direction so that anyhow could reach to India border. On the way he found some smoke and deem light from right site of some hut. Cautiously enough he reached near to hut to survey. The bamboo door was facing Indian border

. He managed to peep inside, could see some Hindu Deity photo where the oil lamp was burning. He sighed for a moment. He stepped further; found the old women was busy in cooking on the wooden fire. He stood for a while but the old lady could hear, without raising her head, easiness in those steps in heavy shoes. Without any fear she asked to that unknown person, "May I know whom you want?" He immediately answered, "I am from Indian army. I lost my way back while returning to Indian border in this darken area. Place is unknown to me. If not mistaken your hut is in the opposite of us I mean next to Indian territory?"

"Yes, son you are judged. We are just near the border. "

"How you dare to stay just near the border and boldly praying Hindu God?" Soldier asked.

"Why to scare for such enemy who ruined my entire family?" Old lady vehemently uttered those words. He could observe her sorrowful wrinkled face in the deem light while uttering those harsh words.

She could observed his gilt on face but none of his, pointed out at a small flat stone, and said, "Be seated there. I will give you some water to cool you down. "

He obeyed her and sat on the stone such way from where he could survey the entire place. While she was on turn to fetch a mug of water, could notice his shroud way of surveillance. But she was not the cause of offensive anymore being his usual duty. She was to reconnect back since was sure about his views, but soldier interrupted, "Would you like to come back to India? I will take care of you. " Eventually she could understand his feeling and narrated her past.

She said, " My dear son, I understood and eventually accepted as there is no one with me here accept this small shelter and nearby jungle from where I bring the food for my survivor. "

Soldier asked since when you were here? You had every reason to cross the border be an India residence.

She replied in very soft words about her origin place of birth and even her all relations who were domicile of the place. They had huge land and big house made out of red bricks. We all together more than 70 people were staying happy life but after partition we have lost everything. We were harassed for some or other reason and had no way but to move out after some of the deaths occurred in front of us. That we about 25 survived decided to shift out of the region but few went back to collect some of those valuables, were killed. Only seven could reached up to here thinking to be safe here and would cross the border any moment. But that time never arrived, they followed us and accused us under some or other reason. That arrest took them to unknown place where so far no one knows their faith. I, many time thought to get rid of all these and shift the place instead of just sitting on border. But again a matter of heart did not allowed me to do so as multiple memories of the place and many happy and emotional moments were with me. That is how the last nearly twenty years were passed here.

Soldier had no words to speak further but wanted to be cautioned herself. He stood attentive but in intention to proceed but old lady did not allowed him. She said, "My son, I advise, not to step out of the house. Any moment enemy would come in search of the left over. This is good time for drug mafia and loot the houses under the pretention of being check-up. I am sure of this, so better you make up your mind to go tomorrow morning that too before sun rise. "

Sinha accepted her advice. He could sense his motherly affection which was missing since long. Early morning he was preparing to go out. While putting on those shoes, he looked at the old lady who was found in tears. Small number of hours was enough for her to have the feel of her son. He departed without saying good-bye but when turned once found the Old lady was virtually broke down against the door.

When soldier was about to reach the border found number of migrants caring their belongings and children in hand. Site was very sorrowful but no way except mourning at the situation created by enemy. The soldier decided his return journey to reach his village. He had many thoughts gathered in his mind, Why this was the war when everything was going well? Our economy was well in control. People were happy enough with their life. Is that China induced the idea to lift communist party in Indian region? Such many questions were raised in his mind. After all he was a soldier at his heart and certain political thinking was beyond his jurisdiction and that's what made him set aside and boarded the train to reach to his destination. Soon after he stepped down from train, found station master in front of him, asked him, "Where were you for last three days? You just loaded your belongings in my office and left without uttering any words? Some of colleagues who came along with you too were unaware your where about. Every day your family members were visiting the office along with many other villagers. They were to report your office. "

Sinha did never expressed his sorry face but the unfair situation and impact on his mind while returning to this place. That prompted him to travel further without any baggage along with him. That was the reason he dumped his bedding in the station masters office so that everyone is aware of his safe arrival. Soon after getting out of train he collected his belongings, instead walking to home place which was nearly 4-5 kilometres away from the station, preferred to sit in duly built open waiting place for a while. Some of the villager spread the news of his safe arrival made many close and dear arrived at station. Some garlanded too. But he refused initially to accept as he was not the part of that war but was on vigilance duty. The colleague who reached the village before him already narrated about his prompt vigilance gave the movant of enemy all along the border made India Army alert without creating war like situation, helped to move all along the border. He was sent to border for various reasons which he could disclose at the moment. Sinha looked curiously at those colleague who gave such information, even unknown to him, had given to his Captain in charge. Great of him. Now he could understood why he was promoted to the rank of Major and he as Captain and included in U. N. Army. He was to report them but only after 4 months when earlier group returns back.

Father with many others came along with bullock cart where as some others came with loaded tractors to receive him. But he refused to climb except loading his own belonging. When all moved out of Railway premises, on the way many youngsters and farm workers left their work and stood on the farms high rise to wave and greet him. That was really emotional moment and love for him while on his walk. Village was nearing, could be sensed by surrounded trees all around. He was on the verge of crossing Small River, bent down to remove his shoes, but was stopped in doing so. He looked at them in question, uttered himself, "My shoes though all proof, but why to deteriorate. I have to take care of those shoes as have to go back with same condition. I have no right to use them when I am in civil code. "

His one of friend said, "Look there, how that bullock cart is passing through the water. Wheels tires hardly merged in water and bull had to bend down enough to drink that water. By the side of river is absolutely dry and walk with little care being almost dried shore. Take care on marshy places, where someone dumped the soil along with river sand. "

He crossed the river looking behind once again those dry banks and green trees still standing safe on it. Sinha was in no mood to speak but yet uttered, "Are anyone is taking care of these trees banking on shore?

Some other day, morning you may find them vanished without any notice. I hope this is responsibility of every villager to keep the place safe from all such negligence. He crossed the Hanuman's Temple where some villagers were sitting under the banyan tree just nearby. Old trees were the great relief for such old and retired villagers. He felt the sigh of relief while reaching the entrance, had casual look to left, sited a small water flow nearly full of black waste water rolling and mixing the clean water of rivulet behind the Temple. He was agonized by the very first site he looked at. . . He was proud of his village for many reason but that site disturbed him.

Soon after getting over the emotional time with family and others, went to his father's farm. That farm was given by Government just after father's retirement from Army. Enough fertile ten acre land near another small revolute was good enough for their survivor. Small revolute were gift from nature through the mountainous area though were far away from that place. He decided to make the situation favourable to suit for additional farming without disturbing his father's land. His approach to Government in authority to borrow an unfertilized land where even sheep had anything to graze there so far. That piece of five acre land which was barren and ideal since ages. Government had no objection to give him as under his custody for trial purpose. Process was to take some time meanwhile he collected some young youth after their work hours. He now became an instructor, giving lessons of physical training on the plain. That was not easy for him to gather and keep them together though he was generous and friendly to them, worked out many war type situations along with many stories. That not only became popular but many other from other age group too joined his scot. Many of themselves arranged some kind of uniform, as if were from army and being trained. That prompted many of them to join army of their own, because of the induced spirit created in them by him.

The five acre land was allotted to him for some specific purpose. Many villagers thought that must be for playing matches or opening private academy for youngsters. He collected some samples from the barren places and even from marshy land in different pouches and marked the locations from where that was collected. All samples were sent to Agriculture research laboratories. He personally stood till report was ready. Most of the places the land was having more percentage of Iron and copper along with lead. How to neutralise all such unfertilized metal was real problem. He marked that specific area. He took some advice from scientist from research institute but was not satisfied being costly affair. That involved the purchase cost of Phosphate and Urea. He then went to gather (the place where cows and buffalos had no owner) where plenty of cow dunk and raw streaks were getting rotten. He added some water to get faster that process. His youngster understood his motive and they too participated to develop the land. But again how to get water to cultivate common vegetables. Many of them wanted to wait till it rains but he was in hurry to get those results. His father too was of the same opinion but he sought out the solution by connecting small waste water streams of all those houses together. He dig out big square of 20 by 20 and 10 feet deep and covered all sides and bottom with waste tarpaulin pasted together. Collected water was treated with acid and then neutralized by caustic till 7-to 8 ph. achieved. All village people together wanted to be part of the project though they were unsure about many unknown things and end results. De-rooting shrubs, dry streaks willows were removed voluntary. Father helped him in Ploughing the land, surfacing and given cart to carry out loading and spreading all organic dry waste collected at dumping place. That was going to work to fertilize the land in all respect. . . Those all such activities were much appreciable and now he felt for the first time the joy of such exploration where the land looked to be ready for planting the seeds soon after the first rain showers. But now he need not wait till then as was the treated water was available.

Time was rapidly flowing and main source were to be boosted by giving physical training to them. That physical training conducted was something different and special for everyone caused to spread the news all over the region nearby. Many of them gave many advices on their casual visit there. Government authorities were also observing the proper utilisation of land prompted to offer another piece of land for cultivation. He was happy to learn the decision and faith shown towards him was once again encouraged further along with that entire colleague. That was celebration day when someone from other village offered tractor for their use. He being from defence learned it immediately for their use and practiced for several hours so that no fuel would waste. Soon he was asked to visit the place that was offered. He, along with others trodden the unknown land, map in hand to know the exact location that was marked by Government official. It seemed some miles away from the present ongoing project. Many doubt arrived while walking through the marshy track full of willows and swampy trees. When they reached the location which was below the topless twin mountains. He immediately though the place good for paddy crops. But how to make the land fertile was the problem. All those interested reached to the strange land and now they all spread around to know the place. Each one was thinking in their own way though they had common goal and what could be done was their common objective. Since the place was inhabited found many places, trees were untouched, possibly even for medicinally useful but growing only at high altitude. He also surveyed some places dotted with pine trees. Because of the group noise silence was broke down, made every one of them look up in the sky as many unknown flyers came out from the distance directions. No trace of any wild animal around. Observation made by Sinha gone curious to understand the situation gone little worried. The project was quite interesting yet challenging could motivate him but worried how far his colleague would sustain in his absence. His privilege leave would not be enough and to keep going such work was really difficult task for him. After all that was the challenge and being from army he never wanted to be dithered by any such reason that he decided. Large area was like a burden to develop for common man, even for youngsters but when such strong army man was with them, deter mind to be part of developing as challenge. That time everyone forgotten their forefront leader would leave the place soon after his pre-village leave that would be over. Everyone started lying demarking the area that was allotted by Government. As soon as the work completed, found the awful darkness covered under the base of those mountain. Many unknown sounds were being heard and stopped soon, had to walk through, taking care at every step ahead.

That situation was unusual even for those villagers. But Soldier was to experience every kind of situation which he and even his friends would face in future. That was the great source of teaching to his co-workers and could proceed to gain the result. That way everyone was the soldier in his own way under common command in present. Captain Sinha once again took out the map and rolled out with the help of other two to check the route they came to this spot, though was not so far, may be less than 3 to 3 1/2 miles from their present project they undertook. The route was then marked by the surveyor in authority knowing the odd and uneven land. Captain saw the earlier route was taken them by the side of some small revolute which has taken too long but safe. But now the evening would lead them somewhere else through the darken *and dense forest. His lighter too went useless while charting out the new and short route. Though he changed the route without the knowledge or any navigator from the known place. They trodden many thorny bushes under their raw shoes. Sometimes plain and some, where land was making their walk difficult, could understood the reason for surveyor's advice for long route. Now Sinha became Captain of that scot, to give direction asked to wait since could heard the moving of some reptile through that marshy land. They waited for some time and went near those thorny plants to break the long branches. Everyone was asked to shuffle those bushes ahead of them so that any creature passes across could make their way safe. Thereafter they found again another hurdle of hard thorny plants. They had to brake them down every possible way and make quite hard work to cross over them, before could reach to their village. Time did not saved but experienced of such emergency they faced and came out from odds. While doing so every once clothes were torn. Every one left to rivulet and cleaned their muddy trousers and injured arms. Captain felt sorry for that who wanted to cut short way but did not repented as was being faced new kind of experience by his colleagues. Before dispersing he smilingly informed to them, "Look my friends. This is how we manage to catch the terrorist or enemy and spy getting when getting out of reach. We are trained practically this way by giving such demonstration on real field. Our movement on the field of war. Many of you are preparing to join army, so take this as first lesson. " Everyone was encouraged by his words hopping for some or other kind of future, even in civil life.*

The other day he went to dump yard where cow dunk and other waste were accumulated. They were shifted to hollow pit and covered with wet and dry soil. That was the way to get waste rotten faster. Another place was found full with waste water as the result of excavated place earlier. Many such ditches were the result of accumulated such water. All hard waste and tarpaulin were spread at bottom to avoid water soak in soil. Task was difficult was done by getting those material from dumping yard lying them at bottom. Captain was caught in duel mind on priorities in front of him. He discussed the issue, asked, "Dear friends, Yesterday we had been to that baron land. Evening time was not enough to know about the land culture and how we turn into fertile one."

One of them suggested, "Let us not forgot it is very difficult to get any land from Government. By virtue of our present work the land was proposed for us. Otherwise that one could been given to any time to anyone close to them. Let us work out on newly proposed land and reach out to future activities. Deal is yet to be finalised. Unless we proceed for some work development on paper, it is likely, would not be offered to us. "

"You are right, but do not forget the work we have taken in hand has to be completed and must show the result too!"

Captain agreed by principle knowing fully the administration work and asked everyone to spread the accumulated water in the entire land. Rain is quite far and we have to reach out to our earlier plan. He said water accumulated was not enough but let us try. Next day he found someone from their team made long ditch to flow the water towards dressed land. They all followed the dug channel through which the water flow could be observed. At one place the excess accumulated water seen by colleague, tried to canalised to side way, where one of them was making trench to collect excess water. Some of them stopped him making such uncalled work, out of his own enthusiastic way. Captain, so called their leader pat him on his shoulder, suggested, "Friend your initiative is appreciated by all of us. Infect I too was to take over this work with help of machine to avoid such laborious work together with spread out heaps of fertilizer like -soda ash and urea. Now it's time to make the land wet so that soaking process would start. By this time we learnt such trench would not help anymore, have to have some other solution. All waste water would have been wasted in the dry soil or even percolate further and all our further efforts would be meaningless. " All others thought Captain might have got agitated by such act though would not show on his face. Instead he learnt and we all learnt something more about the irrigation and soil conservation that would absorb particular amount of water.

When the group went to check the quantity of water collected in the newly made pond, found level had gone down and the newly ditched places were soaked in water. Out of curiosity every one of them went to see how far water reached, found not even a furlong. All of them stood with long faces near the dry channel, but Captain advised them, "Good enough. Now we understood the land has enough capacity to hold the water. Today we make long trench with help of machine. In fact our project was not far from our village, yet there was no owner who had capacity to purchase or reserves funds for special work and fortunately we were lucky enough to hold at the moment. His brain was storming not to lose that opportunity but how to solve the problem to generate flow of enough water that required before the seeds were sowed. Rain was nearby to help or even digging of new water well was beyond their reach in short period. His had hardly had three weeks in hand where he would be able to hand over the running project. Rest of the work was to care normal and common in all respect, provided collected water was properly rationed till rain was to arrive. Some one of them had someone from their close relation would give them bags of cement on loan but he also had little knowledge of mixing some proportion of using large amount of lime instead of cement. Idea was good enough to resolve the water socking problem. Some villagers who was curiously listening their discussion, leaned and came forward to the group, informed, "Can I help you to know the place where lime would be available?"

"Of course. It's our pleaser if some guides us. "

The stranger turned around and pointed out the east end mountain having Lime quarry at its middle. Some vehicle is required to reach and collect those crushed stones. From there, same load is to be taken to another place where grinding to fine particles would follow. Quality of that grinded lime is very good, having binding capacity is as good as fresh cement. You could try at least once. "

Everyone was encouraged by his guidance but Sinha had left with few days to be with them where such task within time was found to be difficult. Though his node in casual way, was definitely thinking otherwise some other option. Evening was usually interesting every day after completion of specific task. They all seat together in circle and discuss next day's task, but today left to their houses, being unusual work ahead, never know how to organise transport at distant places and purchase of lime and crushing cost.

Sinha, in his capacity wanted to give some other thought for the present issue. He walked to the rivulet flowing nearby. Water was quite enough for their use to soak the said land initially till it turned fertile. Evening sun was shining at the west end. As was going down furthermore brilliantly, looked revolving faster and faster. He stunt at the sight, when nature could glow at every stage why human could not. He sat on the nearby stone in silent and roused to the occasion. He walked down along the flow of water till low level was found near the rocky portion. That was like obstacle for the flow, helped to accumulate good amount of water. Many farmers were busy using bucket wheels or water pumps to irrigate their cultivated farms. He returned before late hours of the late evening appeared. He reached the spot where he was seating that evening, to find the place to make a small dam by filling stones and sand laying nearby, allowing some water to run downwards. His idea to save time though was good enough, but possible many other villagers may take objection being stoppage of water and starving others. That was crucial stage of his decision. At one way he was exploring the land for cultivation and other way disturbing others set up of usual work. He reminded how in cities waste water was thrown by gutter and huge cement pipe. Even to have such method evolve money. Bamboo too are costly that way. People would destroy bamboo jungle once used by us. The last and best could be plastic pipe could work in always. Very next day he along with others reached to manufacturer who helped him with readymade one and was great help when he delivered it at free of cost. Matter was solved after lying down those pipes in the place. Everyone was hurry to start the pump and irrigate the place. Captain was happy at the result, knowing rest of the process was well known to all these youngster even better than him, so asked to finish entire job including sowing and nurturing. People though were happy but felt nervous, as he is likely to be away in few days. Very next day Sinha went near the tractor and checked all accessory intact. He himself sat and taken test drive found some of those wheels jarring, possibly brought from junk yard. He oiled almost every part and was aware, had once again gone out for long trial. That because he was aware that the other land which was given on lease was quite far. He had to pass all those odds and marshy places to reach there. He did not know how the machine would stand on slanted portion and also river cross over. Though he was comfortable at present, but thought to have someone with him in case of brake down. Now he decided to plain the given land and demark it before ploughing. That was pleasant experience to make ride on tractor with any smooth or even rough surfaces. They were nearing to place just after crossing the river. River was definitely was shallow, had sensed with thick mud inside and likely to stuck anywhere anytime. He had no option but drive carefully but faster than average speed. Tractors wheel stuck at some big stone had to revert the wheel and restart. They almost were touching to the shore, tractor slipped and tilted. His fellow colleague could hold his seat, but Sinha who was steering fallen from tractor. His leg was under the tractors chassis, was shouted but no use as no one was there except the poor fellow who had no capacity to help him except shouting around. He immediately ran back, virtually shouting. The silent place had many echo, could be heard by nearby villagers in numbers rushed in the direction from where shouts appeared. Many of them instead predicting anything moved out with iron rods and wooden streaks. They saw the man running to some other direction was called back and went with him at the place of accident. Site was not easy to go inside where only Sinha's head could been seen, just above muddy water. Some villagers went other side of the rivulet to tilt the tractor to opposite side. It was very difficult to understand how far Sinha was under bonnet of engine. It was very essential to lift the tractor with the help auto lift, instead pulling it as it might injure further or some other organ of

Sinha's body. For that someone has to enter the pond with bigger stone, could be lodged over to, stand on it. That would give enough pressure to push it to other side. In the process many other villagers joined to collect bigger stone laying outside the pond and fill the some part of muddy place, so that many of them could add pressure unitedly to lift the portion of it. Efforts together could help to bring the tractor just on the bank of pond. But they all found Captain Sinha was unable to come out of sticky and muddy location. Some of them brought bigger bamboo and pushed to Sinha, whose efforts succeeded by pushing his foot against the hard surface under his foot. He, the Captain spun around on his heel and fronted us, all the brown mud had gone out of his face and even though his nose was blue and was looking like a ghost. Everyone felt sorry to see him in the form but tired. He was taken to nearby well with others help but midway refused and walked down alone and took the bath. Even from that distance he could see the entire villagers were busy cleaning the tractor which too was full of mud. Sinha's dumbness was merge with the moment and regain the strength and walk down towards the tractor that was being made ready. By this time those villagers could get the reason and the work he has undertaken. They themselves wanted to be the part of the project that he wanted to develop. Sinha casually checked some part of engine out of many doubts in his mind but determined to sit on a wheel and powered the engine without moving further. He stepped down and oiled the wheels. That was spur of the time to show his courage to those strange dwellers from nearby hamlet who saved his life from drowning in the sticky mud. Now it was his turn to lead them for his future requirement. Sinha, even at that exciting moment, sat at the tractor wheel and powered the engine and thrown the gear forward, moved with some surged by jerk, brought instantly out from the marshy place. His brain stormed for the moment as he was to get away from his earlier colleague if he would take any sort of help from these new group of people. He driven that tractor to some distance in confirmation for its immediate utilization and surfaced piece of small portion of land. Surfacing of the land was priority to get trust, confidence and co-operation of those villagers, though were strangers. Their dwelling thereby near to place would help in near future. Though they became proud of him who had taken a challenge to make the strange land fertile. They were proud when they heard from someone, they might have heard the blessed things and grumbled over his passion completely, but taken over by bold initiative they all decided to help him but later on someone threatened him in horrible terms. Before anything could happen some sound came from the top of the hill whose horse was galloping through the plane fortunately that was belong to the said group who had threatened him. That was the reason those miscreant had to leave the place, followed after the horse. It looked to Sinha this is the last signal of danger turned away in other direction they had deserted in fear, panic out of revenge for their words. Captain knows now nothing is remained when people nearby hamlet who came running and made the rescue operation. Surprisingly a horse rider came inside and swept with full gallop down the slope. Same rider along with many others horse rider came up and tried to sweep those people with some kind of sharp weapons to stop the development of the land. But by this time the many dwellers nearby hamlets were already prepared to take the revenge of earlier attack. In the process of their fight one of the horse riders collapsed upon his face and barely saved by his co-rider. Before any major attempt was expected to take place they fled away from the spot. Over the time Sinha got giddiness and was to fell down from where he was standing. Someone's lead promptly put him on tractors seat and drove to city hospital which was far, about 8-10 km's. By this time his pain at the left leg found unbearable. On the way one trailer full of hay was passing through, had given a help to connect to theirs tractor. He was laid down at ease who too had nap on the way. On admission was given some treatment, but Doctor declared a fracture below knee would make him difficult to have a normal walk. Doctor was on his side, given a Letter to his defence head quarter about his sickness and the fractured leg. He declared of his unfitness to work for another two and a half month.

Sinha being from defence asked to provide a sick certificate along with the letter to be it to his head quarter. Few days later he could be released from hospitalization, but advised to avoid any work at least for another 3-4 months thereafter.

Along with his friends he return to home where his parents never allowed to get him out of the house. Every morning all those people used to gather at his house to enquire about the accident and the injury that he revived. Someone remarked that Sinha should have never operated such a junk tractor that was laying in the scrap yard. On hearing such a remark from unknown villager he calmly reverted back to those who flashed such a remark towards the tractor which had already worked for his initial project. He explained to them, it was his wrong judgement in assessing the place before crossing the rivulet where muddy and sluggish pond situation could have seen. Every day was as bright as before when he found the work at both end were progressing beyond his expectation. Those strangers though were UN accustomed dwellers in handling such uncalled and tough situation but were helpful in their every capacity. Surprisingly similar customised eating habits helped them to build up togetherness was the need of the time. That's what Captain was searching and destined their togetherness as appeared. Now Sinha had enough time to collaborate them for various reason. New land was developed had enough water for irrigation.

Sandy land was because of the water rolling down from the mountain at its hill stock. . All through, water flow was rushing down also with good soil, was much needed to makeover the land. Tree plantation was taken in hand to avoid any further erosion of soil after makeover. Only five acres were used for plantation and rest five acre for producing rice. Before rain likely to begin, they put all efforts to be within the seasonal range. Captain Sinha released from the hospital on his advocacy of being far away the place. But doctor was reluctant to do so. Sinha argued doctor saying, "Reason to do so is because my ongoing project require my regular consultancy for the colleague who are working so hard!" rest of the explanation was further given by his close friends who were around him. Doctor understood the entire episode where the captain was leading the entire team at two places. He was not discharged from the hospital but allowed to be in house with some precaution. He was given an arm rest to be used while walking. For few days he could not exert. Every day morning all his colleagues used to gather there in his house said to be a large drawing room for regular meeting and getting direction for the work to be completed for the day. Captain was really happy for the two reasons. His initial project looked to be successful after being led the plastic pipes to irrigate water from treated sump to the field where were seeds sawn. It was only now the minimum period require for the shoots to protrude from the cultivated land and second one the new barren land at the bottom of the hill would be workable. . . Though was far away but was worth developing being used by some miscreant for uncivilized purpose. Those people were headache for administration as whole. Every days progress was noted by many district around, made them aware of the cause wanted to follow the pattern of work, but who will bell the cat was the problem. After all that was social work without any benefit as such but to see the pretty good site was the matter for all those who speak about the individual. It seemed media had taken care by some article alerted many social workers. One of the foreign media lady gone to Army head quarter to get some of the information about one of the Solder (Captain) was doing some extra ordinary work for those villagers. She could have reached direct to the concerned person, but being from India Army, taken precaution and requested someone from them to join with her. They arranged Sinha's immediate boss Major Shrikhande under whom he was trained. Major was on special duty yet was released for few days to be with her and also to know the purpose of her visit and to know Sinha's welfare and extension of leave. They reached the village which was far from the main city and had to hire horse cart being raw road. They had to get down outskirt of the said village being led through the narrow passage. While turning down to the place they found his big house and strong pillars and beams under which large space for strangers to rest, and large water pot at one side. Adjoining drawing room was the sign of rich farmer who equipped with all city facilities. One of their team member pointed out many photos of Army people holding ranks and medals on their chest. He remarked while going through all those photo's, "Why was need to serve Army when they themselves having such good land with them. " One of the house member vehemently replied, "For Nations Cause Madam, " That touched Major who was real commander by heart but did not uttered a single word. But observed mild smile from Sinha's father who too retired from the Army, treated them with necessary breakfast, after their hazardous travel. That was afternoon and wanted to return back to catch their train were taken to trail project where villager's participation was crucial. One of the supporter from Tehsil, took initiative to explain in detail about the land that was neglected since long. "Some unknown person interfered, asked, "Why such fertile land that to near to this village was left without using for the purpose?" Heuristic replied in his own way, "You are absolutely right. Today you see this land is most useful but earlier many farmers tried and finally abundant only to use as dump yard. Sinha who came on his pre village leave, before being appointed as Captain for Peace keeping force from India, who thought of doing some experiment to make the land fertile. He sent the soil for chemical analysis, found quite good quantity of Iron and oxide together which do not allow to grow the seed after few day of sowing. Again he found the source of waste water being drained and evaporated without any utilization. He connected all those drain water sources at one place and also diverted to hollow dump already existed. To avoid waste of extra water, many small dump were made and connected to each other. He also took precaution to all those dump portion were covered by waste tarpaulin to avoid seepage. "

"How dirty and polluted water could be used for the paddy eatable used by human. "

All water is filtered and treated by acid and then buy caustic. This treatment called neutralization of all kind of chemicals. That resulted in salt which was settled in on large tank and water is used even for drinking. If you want we will taste it. "

"That means without using well, bore or river water one can use this water which is available in all season. "

"Yes! Bore water could vanish any time and no guarantee of well water, could dry after rainy season also. "

Sinha's father found busy knowing about his son for whom many visitors were arrived. , asked him not to go far, yet he was not found at spot. Major asked his where about who was aware about his sickness a fraudulence wasn't. If so they would have not learnt through the published news, applaud all through about him and his family.

Someone was arriving from the direction where new project was to take place. But everyone was knowing that after his accident no one had been there. But father was knowing one person who was visiting him regularly, soon after villagers daily meeting was over. Who must be that person, definitely not from our group? He decided to ask the horse rider about his son who was limping while on walk. Otherwise also father was to hold his horse on that spot after noticing large group followed behind him. He thought something serious had happened. It seemed all were in search of that lame man who was helping his hamlet dwellers. Though he stopped the ridding further, kept guessing at everyone there. Major could understood that he does not want to spell out the fact, being brought in odd situation to the Sinha who was at his utmost revolutionary stage of developing the land they needed for many purposes. Major asked him to step down from the horse and tried to understand from the gentlemen, "will you please tell us how far the place from here where his development work in progress. I could read from your face something more about him. I feel he is lame and cannot walk without help of shoulder arm rest." On this the gentlemen said that he's not in a capacity to work with us but guide us by stalling himself somewhere nearby us. Moreover his presence encouraged us. Today morning he arrived and saw all of us doing some fencing work around the large periphery of the land. He did not like that kind of raw fencing help to mend it at some places. Our togetherness could mend entire fencing within few days so that any work carried out inside the land would not be disturbed by any external forces including animals. On hearing all those words of creation made everyone surprise as his act was unknown to them. Major was really proud of him on hearing horse rider would bring him here to meet us. Accordingly horse rider turn back living his work aside. While moving he explain to those people gathered there that exploration of this site was uninhabited. Full of willows and swampy trees. Tract of about 3-4 miles is also marshy and some places uneven, vote tech about one and half to two hours till the river. But none of them were aware of the condition of the river and its downward flow accepts those hamlet dwellers. Horse rider also did not given any info about the place where his Captain's accident took place. The reason behind it was given on Captain's instruction. The group standing over there kept looking at the horse rider felt someone would have joined with him to bring Sinha as help. The major informed the lady journalist "Mam, it would take hours to reach Sinha here till then let us go to his house as it appear evening would follow soon. This place is difficult to walk even by raw and rough walk way. " Journalist looked at Sinha's father in question who to agreed and asked her "ma'am you have to be with us and spend the entire night in our house along with all your colleague and major too|" Major too accepted to be there as guest till overnight. As the time passed Sinha arrived on a horse and with someone's help step down from the saddle. The man followed on the other horse gave him his arm support and helping to reach their balcony. From the window it was almost quite dark everywhere accept deem light could be seen from lantern to show him way to show him way to step up the veranda from where he could locate through the window the group busy discussing some issue. Govt. man who was with them so long stood up intending to come out from the wide open door met Sinha. The gentlemen introduced himself to Sinha and updated today's events taken place in the farm project. He took lead after congratulating his unusual successful work. Sinha insisted him to give a chance to treat him as a guest along with others tonight. Officer said, "I am on official duty and has to report on duty tomorrow for another planned work. I am very much thankful to you for these cordial invitation. "

Sinha entered the house when dinner was being served. Soon on appearance of Sinha in, house made everyone stand. They all stood at their placed to honor him. He too reciprocated in same way and set aside as the dinner was going on. Soon everyone was made comfortable during the night but were curious about many other things including the second project. Early morning was quite pleasant since through the mild cool wave. They found Sinha on a terrace sitting quite facing east before the beginning of sunrise. He found to be relax while in meditation as he always used to tell his collogues very powerful tool that help clear once mind, reconnect to one self, grow as a person. Everyone who had been there appreciate his qualities, grow as industrial, got a new vision of thinks to balance energy and get ready for new challenges. Without disturbing Sinha all went down to have a pre-planned breakfast arranged by family members when, Sinha too came down and prepared to take all those observers and press reporters at the site. As they already had been to all those places in sequence till the ongoing project which was partly completed. Morning dews were shining everywhere on those seeds protrude. The day before horse rider inform his fellow dwellers from hamlet, regarding arrival of the news reporters. Initially they were taken back at the news that heard regarding such visitors but soon recovered to understand their visit was to give them recognition for the work they have under taken. That prompted themselves to prepare a rough road. Overnight Bamboo Bridge was ready and connected by road to nearby village. Major took the reporters team to the prime location of a project where reporters found all those volunteers were doing exercise. To their surprise they all were in half trousers, shirts but many of them without canvas shoes. They soon lined up and saluted them when reached nearby. Major though was surprised at their honor, reciprocated in similar way. Captain Sinha explained them this discipline drill helped them to work together and prepared for defense test. "I am sure many of them would definitely work for defense services. " Major Shrikhande replied immediately who was overwhelmed by their group activities. Major immediately looked at Captain in acceptance and assured their services if qualified for the test. . . When every one of them were busy to understand the way they altogether working, saw the horse rider was approaching near to them, possible to guide them to nearest manageable way. Rider advised, "Look at this rout ahead. All through is bumpy and dusty and both sides covered by thorny shrubs around could scratch their limbs and clothes. " On his advice, they changed the rout. While on the way, companion was telling to Sinha that previous way would take less time but would be better than earlier one. Soon two horse cart arrived. Cart rider jumped out from the cart and went to Sinha who was the only one known to him, said, "Sir, our people arranged this cart for you all to avoid walking through dusty raw route. " Those reporter felt some relief being taken to the place where they were to report about the strange place. On the way rotten smell made everyone uneasy. That nauseous smell felt like returning back. But cart rider assured them, "Sir, very small patch to cover, till then please try to bear or keep your nose cover with handkerchief. Please do not get disturbed by the site. You may see some unusual cases on the way. " Rider's expression appeared in reality when they saw many half burnt animal bodies lying scattered, thronged by many vultures around. Another place they had to pass where partially buried bodies in the ditch, were again unearthed. Site was terrible but Major was confident about Captains capability to overcome all such unruly site to natural environment. Sinha looked at those reporters, too overwhelmed being first time onlooker at that site. That was the reason he always used another route to reach the place where development work was in progress. He assured them definitely to find out some solution to stop such miscreant act. " Cart rider supported, "This would be possible once the project work is succeeded and people start using this road on regular basis. " Sinha replied, "Yes friend, we will work out some scheme that would benefit for all". It appeared the hazards travel was over. Clean breath was possible as grass vapors could be sensed. Someone pointed out the tractor standing at far near the tree but other end of the river. Now they reached the place where temporary Bamboo Bridge was specially made for them to cross over the rivulet. Holding each other's hand could crossed the bridge, sighted reaching at its end. That location was really important place for those reporters came in group. They wanted public to know how to use abundant land for once benefit when many people were starving many other places. It was so pleasing day for Sinha being saved by those dwellers and some of his own efforts from terrible accident. Now he felt first time the joy of exploration when nothing raw was left in front but plain land. Major began to enjoy himself, looked around with some interest on the strange land. One could visualize the combine efforts could realize the dream Sinha saw in them. Major thrown his eyes all over the land, saw neatly converted plain where as other places were yet as raw as of ancient year. He was sure of him would think to enhancement it further was not out of his capacity. Many field workers were left their work to see those new visitors and a white women looked to be foreigner for them. They never came in contact with such personalities who would work for them in some or other way.

Lady reporter asked, "Why the land is divided in two parts?"

Question raised every once mind but they lost in the ground reality, the large site of land is ready for cultivation. Sinha explained them, "Upper slanting land is getting eroded in rains. When it rains heavily it's getting eroded. This place have good quality of soil, but every year's erosion would make it barren. Large number of tree plantation would definitely not only stop erosion but would fetch money too. Rest five acre land will be used for cultivating ground nuts."

"Why not for paddy rice? It looks better for that."

"You are right but that is long process where as ground nut would be easy comparatively. Once it grown fully, plants could be pulled out, dried and ground nut could be separated and sold directly to market. "'

Major was aware by that time when Sinha would not be available to see the result, being away from the country. He took Sinha aside and asked for extension in his leave. Group was aware of that he was on leave and who would take the charge of such critical work said to be difficult for these dwellers? Apart from that the land is quite away from those other villages where connectivity is difficult. Sinha could read their mind explained, "I know, you might be thinking what could happen if I am away after few days. For that I already made these people to mingle with others by helping each other. They need not employ those whom, who would migrate from other places for such work. Sinha, called one of them who was strong and broad shouldered and round in face, "Would you like to serve in Army? But for that you have to pass some of the examination and go under tough training. " He was happy to learn but Sinha got confuse by his sudden decision on such tribal who settle and scattered nearby hamlet. They did not have even minimum standard qualification to get through the examination. Major put his hand on Sinha's shoulder, "Not to worry we will educate them till then they could be given some other work which need not have any qualification. If they are interested guide them and help in applying for it. " Sinha, never thought his work could be extended to such stage. These tribal were fit for very hard work and found to be strong headed by Major. While leaving the place group congratulated him and backward dwellers, asked them to place a board at every entrance of villages, written on it ~ JAY JAWAN – JAY KISAN. . . "People only speak about that slogan given by Late Lal Bhahadur Shashriji, but here you are the one practiced in all respect, shown the way of application. We all are impressed by the work and their interest in Indian Army. We all would display such board at everywhere in possible way, because it's need of the time. " Everyone did not forget the Tahsildar of the region never returned to show them second project was being carried out and was far away in the strange land? Someone was worried whether those official get the land ready for use and get reed of any criminal activities in that region? Are they using these innocents for their own benefit? Major decided to write in details some plan to head of the government. But kept as secret for the time being! Those people there arranged all kind of transport to carry them to the railway station, waited too till train departed.

Captain was in hurry to organize all those people working in two projects would mixed them and work together as close as possible. He was aware, their close working would leap the effective community as in total would get better result. That was crucial day when he received a warrant to join the second batch, consisting of nearly 200 soldiers, were ready to go other country under the Government of India's instruction to join Peace keeping force in east. It was really hard time for everyone there to work without his guidance, but were also trained to mix with each other and know the different stages at which one has to cultivate. As communication was increased more and more land was cultivated. Captain Sinha made arrangement in such a way that water flowing from mountain was directed at its both ends by dumping number of boulders to prevent the rich soil being washed out. Thereby water collected at the base was turned into pond and could be used by everyone nearby for their miner irrigation. Togetherness not only helped them all but minimized internal rivalry. Exchange of tools, accessories and machinery helped all together to cultivate 15 acres of land.

Captain Sinha was already on board and the flight was delayed for some unknown reason. They all landed at the airport and were ready to take out their luggage, found some unknown group attacked them with guns. It seemed since the news was already with management there, alerted Airport security guards, and attacked them and corrido red by vans in corral till Indian troop reached to their vehicle standing near the gate. That was sudden attack but need not say so as their flight was delayed for the same reason. They thought they made all safety arrangements but never know from where those attackers entered or changed their attire. Indian troops were on alert thereafter, went in the attacking attitude to save themselves. That worked, as they tried to rout short, the mob equipped with rife was already stationed there could understood some military action was to take place. Their readiness stopped the train of vehicles on the thicket, started firing immediately on them. Captain Sinha was already sensed, instructed quite in advance, jumped out of van, along with gun and rifle with bonnet. It was mistaken by those terror group, gone hay way and scattered, were cot by India army. No great efforts but the courage displayed by each one of them had no choice but left their arms on the way. Many of them were got custody were handed over to the Government who were appointed by U. N. Today they all were taken to the place where large firing base surrounded by those more than 50 barracks, mess and interment hall. Sinha felt ridiculous about the hall at middle of barrack or otherwise some secret place for government itself to know the movement of U. N. deployed troops? He went around to find out the strong room for ammunitions and weapons which was wide opened near the hall itself. He changed the place for all weapons and ammunitions next to him where that would be under his observation. For outsiders, he made the feel of strong room filled with weapons. He was aware such places are always under scan by terrorist and likely to be attacked. The day was passed in arranging all their needs, though were alerted by Captain. Next day morning he saw one young boy wondering around, had been near strong room which was locked but without any sentry to guard. Captain without delay arranged some guard outside, keeping some dummy rifle inside. Before sunset he took some of his colleague along with him in civilian dress. They walked through some small portion of jungle and reached at the vegetable market which was full in varieties of vegetables, fish and pig mutton on their shelves. But most of them arranged goods on spread over of some plastic yards. Quite big market where some of them thought of purchasing fruits for themselves. Sinha was remained on lookers for the overall activities, saw the same boy was following them. As the group was busy in purchasing, he rushed to the last vender and stood in, was speaking with him. The vender just cast a glance at the site made Captain alert, asked others to windup the purchasing faster, being without any protective devices with them, except Captain being in civil code. No one were aware of the reason, but on the way he asked to be always be ready for any unwarranted situation. Next day same boy was found with milk van supplier, stormed his brain in appreciation of his courage for his repeated attempt to find out the storage of Arm and Ammunitions. Captain tried to recapture yesterday's visit. He noticed all those venders were farmers from nearby villages and that was the main source of their earning. At the same time he saw boy was friendly with many of them that also indicating those villagers were working for government in their own way that also mean, they do not believe anyone of them? Something was confusing to him, hence he decided to send some of his close one who also worked as secrete agent for them earlier. He suggested to him to get latest information whether any change in government policy and collect some magazines from book stalls. He was not to travel at stretch but cautious enough to understand those views of common people on the way. Capital was not far away but he could map those political activities and connectivity in between them. This observation likely to take at least three -four days meanwhile Sinha had arranged many small attempts to go to nearby places. People respecting those new comers or visitors to their places. . . Main occupation seemed the farming, cultivation and selling in the nearby market. They crossed over the market and some of those villages through rough and dusty road. From distance they located another crowded place, where buffalos and cows were sold. Money in Rio or French dollar were seen for exchange. At some distance again vegetable and fish market was at sight, which was slipped, returned through another road which passes through another thick jungle by narrow way, saw the river full of water, and trees on shore had to bent over that water being dense trees around. They heard some rustle inside those trees, where two women were laying in occult position, barely half wore clothes. Soldiers went nearby to help them but refused to take any help. Some dead wood were lying nearby for once use were found scattered all the way.

Sinha understood everything, asked his soldiers to collect them together and make wind up in bunches. That experience was awful not to be repeated elsewhere by anyone of them.

The Indian soldier was get lot many information before he could reached to the city library. He collected some of old books and some magazines along with latest newspaper. His tiredness made him seat on the garden bench but saw one of the white couple was going inside the restaurant, followed them as if in search of clean water. Soldier was uneasy while seating nearby them, brought courage to talk himself, "Hello, I am also visitor wanted to have some food before going to temple. " The French lady said, " for that you have to book in advance and start early morning being the largest Hindu Vishnu Temple in the World. " That was the news for him but did not wanted to visit being was on different task. Just to satisfy them he replied, "Yes, I will do so on the next visit. " He continued, "How is the country's people you find here. That way I am India, just came as tourist along with my friend and since he was sick did not joined me. "

"Good enough, " Said French man. Said further, "My ancestors were here for many years and had good houses and properties, but as years passed changed the political situation and entire valued properties were taken by many strangers, even government did helped them. We are here again to go through those old memories and many other changed civilization. "

"Yes I was told by many of villagers and people from small town how rapidly people were changing their mind and polities the situation. . . " "I too experienced those people who are today with government would change their mind and support army who had acted against the government. "

"Reason behind that because of King who is head of state. Many occasions he takes help from army in case he decides to dissolve the parliament. King had right to deputy assistant to look into political affairs but if somebody overrule him he takes army support along with public. "

Soldier struggled while speaking his doubt about the U. N. Peacekeeping force for civilian use. Fights among those group would never know to whom to support. "

French man who had experienced, regretful about the matter, vehemently uttered, "Look my friend I know you are Indian and Indian Army was already deployed by U, N. Peace keeping force. Because of this Cambodian Civil War- while the 1967 insurgency unplanned, Khmer tried, All PAUN/ Viet. Cong forces were to withdraw from Cambodian soil within 72 hours. Last minute efforts on the part of the U. S. to arrange peace agreement. " Infantry battalion from India served by rotation in UN. . . Emergency Force to ensure the withdrawal of France, U. K. and Israel from the Egyptian territory and to sustain the peace between Israel and the Arab neighbors. . 27 Indian and UN Peace Keepers lost their lives in this operation. "

Soldier sat down in surprise, asked the French man seating along with the lady, "How do you know all those details?"

He who became friendly by that time explained to him, " I was part of it and reached to Captain Level by the better performance of mine. . . I wanted to go through just a common visitor here along with my wife who too was eager to know the Cambodian which was rich like India where gold, silver and pearl were used as currency in exchange. . . The very first century the India Brahmin from south arrived here and married to Nag Rani. They formed a kingdom by name ~~~~. The livelihood was very hard and he planned many small and large scale water dams to hold the water and began to cultivate rice all over. He ruled here for 600 years. There after the king Combo was ruling for more than 300 years. People were prospering economically. They form the education, system like old age in Indian style. They built Ganesh Temple and Vishnu temple and followed Hindu religion. Today more than 97% Hindu are scattered all over but mostly on the east north river coast. " French man's wife was calmly heard, wanted to say something but did not interfered, since she too worked in Medical core. It was getting late and repeated ordering of snack dishes would disturbed the restaurant owner.

Otherwise also customers were never allowed to discuss on any political affair, had to came out of restaurant. While departing French man asked him to drop down at the hill top where his earlier Hindu friend who worked with him during the war.

"Pretty good. That means you could still maintained those relations. "

"We are friends since long that was the reason I could stay with him also share information being I was also land holder once here. . . Anyway, where had you been lodged? "Asked French man.

"In fact undecided so far, but kept my small airbag at one of the cottage. They are maintaining lockers for such tourist on hire for some hours. Place may not be fit to pass the night but is near the town. " Soldier replied.

"O. k. I suggest one affordable place with one of the Indian family who will help you to accommodate in their guest room. "

Soldier extended his faith in him and went to the place he had suggested.

Next early morning he was to prepare to go out with the French man to visit the temple at the place where they were to go further. Soldier had wonderful occasion to be with the couple who was sharing lot many information about the country and people, but cautioned about those baggers and pick picketers. Though the soldier was ready early in morning and was waiting for couple till they reach there. While wondering in that compound, saw two police vans passed by. Out of curiosity he came out of the gate to know further, found another car turned left side and stopped near him. He was smart enough to make it confirmed without, moving an inch from the place, looked insider. To his surprise the French man along with his wife was sitting inside. Both came out and walked with him inside the house where they were greeted. French man informed his friend ~~~, "I saw two police vans were running towards the city. Is there anything serious about?"

"Yes, some troops from North West frontier were inside but they all went underground. Their plan to assassinate the King was failed. That was because of those common people. That specific day the fisherman was there to deliver something saw those unusual people with arm made him to go inside and alerted those guards. Common people from the land were supporting King and also helped to maintain the peace. Every kind of efforts failed from outsiders when North-west try to disturb the present government. "

Soon Frenchman asked to line up in que, as only few thousands visitors were allowed inside the Temple, till he parked his vehicle. While on their way here, around the site Frenchman was eager to tell him many aspect of this temple. The temple best known as Angkor Wat. That Southeast Asian country with capital Phnom Penh, Angkor Wat temples ruins and beaches. That massive temple with ornate necklaces design. Just few minute later he took out his camera. He was editor for some foreign magazine and wanted to give them update. One of the lady from western was sitting in front of some Pundit who performed some HAVAN followed by prayer for her good health and prosperity and was preaching while winding red thread on her right hand. It looked entire Hindu way of performing the prayer went unnoticed by the lady and monk moving around. . . We passed them instead asking anything about the ritual, being required to cover quite large area of temple. Long, nicely carved lobbies and many places Indian Psara were neatly carved and well finished in Indian style. Big carved pillars were reminding India Architect. At the center God Vishnu was most impressive sign along with Ganesh Temple. Hours passed, friends wife asked to take rest at the small lake where she served us with some snacks. By that time French man's photo session was over and we boarded the car for the next place known as Temple of Preach VI hear – Ancient, well preserved Hindu temple. Royal Palace temple with jeweled Buddha's statue. On the way we saw Bryon Temple-Angkor Thom Temple carved figures in smiling faces and lastly Ta Prom Temple ruins, overgrown trees around. There were more than 300 temple around the city which were built by earlier Hindu King. As ages passed the Hindu statues and faces being turned in Buddha area.

French man was so much enthusiastic about the history and his wife too was much interested to hear, had no escape, but listen further. Soldier was aware about his limitations yet wanted to know more and more. He suggested to take some coffee on the way before he was to depart.

Informed about the Khmer Empire- which was established by the 9 the century. The decline continued through the transitional period of approximately 100 years followed by the middle period of Cambodian history, also called the post- Angkor period beginning in the mid of 15 the century. .

Cambodian's culture has its roots in the 6 the centuries in state called Fun am, which is also the oldest. Indianite state in south-east Asia. Fun am gave way to the Angkor Empire with rise the power of King Jayavarman Second in AD 802.

The following 600 years saw powerful Khmer Empire with the rise to power of King Jayavarman Second in AD 802. Powerful King dominated much of the present day Southeast Asia, from border of Myanmar east to South China Sea and north to Laos.

Cambodian language, part of Mon-Khmer family, evolved during that period. It contains elements of Sanskrit, the classical language of Hinduism and Buddhism. Historians have noted that Cambodian can be distinguished from their clothing –checkered scarves know as Karmas are worn instead of straw hat. It was during that period that the Khmer King built the most extensive constructions of religious temple complex. That complex converts 400 sq. Km. contains more than 1080 temples across the country.

The most successful of Agrarian Kings, Jayavarman 1st, Suryavarnam 2nd and Jayvarman 6th, also devised master pieces of ancient engineering, a sophisticated irrigation system that includes a number of bray – that means lakes and canals which insured three rice crops a year. Part of the system is still in use.

As Angkor period ended, Cambodian Capital moved to Longman, the end to Outdoing, was finally to the present capital of Phnom-Penh. Among the main feature of Angora era, besides the movement of the Theravada Buddhism, illustrated in Temple carvings, where Buddhist features gradually replaced Hindu features.

The 15 to 17 the centuries represented a time of foreign influence, when expansionist Siam and Vietnam fought over Cambodia. By the mid – 1800's Cambodia, like most other countries in Asia came under increasing pressure from European Colonial powers. In 1863 King Norodom signed a protectorate Treaty with France.

Buddhism was introduced in the 12th century during rule of Jayavaram 6th. However the Kingdom, then known as Kabuga, fell into decline after Jayavarams region and was nearly annihilated by Thai and Vietnamese invaders Kabuga's power. Kabuga's power steadily diminished until 1863, when France colonized the region, joining Cambodia, Laos and Vietnam into single protectorate known as French. The French quickly up surged all but ceremonial powers from monarch, Norodom when he died in 1904. French passed over his sons and handed over the thorn to his brother, SiSwati. SiSwati and his son, Sihanouks, was elevated to power. Sihanouk's coronation along with Japanese occupation during the war worked to reinforce a sentiment among Cambodians that the region should be free from outside control. After world war 2nd Cambodian sought independence but France was reluctant to part its colony. Cambodian sought independence within the French union in 1949. But French – Indochina war provided an opportunity for Sihanouk to gain full military control of the country. He abdicated in 1955 in favor of his parents, running head of the government and when his father died in 1960, Sihanouk became head of the state without returning the thorn. In 1963 he sort a guarantee of Cambodia's neutrality from all parties in the Vietnam War.

However, North Vietnamese and Vietcong troops had begun using eastern Cambodia as a safe haven from which to launch attacks

Into South Vietnam, making indigenous communist guerrilla movement known as the Kheer Rouge also began to pressure on the government in Phnom Penh. On March 18, 1970, while Sihanouk was abroad, anti – Vietnamese riot broke out and Sihanouk was abroad overthrown by Gen. Lon. The Vietnam peace agreement stipulated withdrawal of foreign forces from Cambodia but fighting continued between Hanoi-based insurgents and U. S. -supplied government troops.

(Cambodia joins the world Trade Organization Elections in July later in 2003, resulted in a stalemate had to form coalition government.

In July 2008, Enesco, the culture of the United State Nations designated the Preach VI hear temple, which sits on the Cambodian side of the Cambodian- Thai border as a U. N. World Heritage site.

One notably Southeast Asian aspect of Tamil Hinduism is the festival of Thaipusam, while other Hindu religions festivals such as Diwali are also well deserved by Hindus in the region. In Thailand and Cambodia, Thai Khmer-language, also called Cambodian Mon-Khmer language spoken by most of the population of Cambodia where it is official language and by some 1. 3 million people in southeastern Thailand and also more than a million people in southern Vietnam.

Khmer is written in on ancient alphabetic script that has the same Indic origins as the script of neighboring languages.)

Few countries have experienced such a harrowing period in their history as Cambodia or Kampuchea, has over the last quarter century. Once the center that of a powerful empire that controlled much of the present day Thailand and parts of the Laos and Vietnam, this former colony has in the more immediate past, been victim of civil war, massive aerial bombardment, a genocidal revolution and foreign occupation, these horrors left profound scars upon the century and its people and even now more than a decade after the expulsion of Khmer Rouge region, Cambodia's future remains far from certain.

Traditional Cambodian literate written in verse, includes both works adopted from India sources and works of indigenous origin. Prose fiction became popular in the early 1950 s, but could scarcely claim to be bookstalls were full of novels and comics and fiction.

The entire day was spent where the time of departure arrived, giving assured visit in near future was greatly admired. Soldier decided to leave them but the French man asked to board the car in intention to help him to reach the same boarding. That night was looked quite warm but some of roaring band of vehicle passed by. French man was not seen in anymore in surprise and was even looked worried. It seems that was a regular guerrilla moment and were knowing fully to whom to attack. Soldier was dropped at the place but French man waited till he reached in the house safely. Soldiers mission of collecting all the information was nearly looked over and next day he was to leave the boarding. Man in charge of the house asked him to be with them till noon and would leave the place only after lunch. Reason was unknown to him but he obeyed and left the house only after noon. He decided to walk through and on the way he could see many industries around. Many workers and activities including some small business shops were made the way at ease. It was quite like normal Indian market place. He waited at some places to have a cup of tea and rest for a while. Some other workers too in group, occupied those chairs were looked discussing their issues. Some of them found furious about unsafe process and more working hours to complete their assignment for export which were mostly to Europe. Some of them raised the question about going to labor court would solve our working conditions. The other one said "If we do so they would displace us by employing youngsters and even below 18 years children. "

"We can fight with management till we are working here there after we will lose our rights"

"What rights? The court is only for name sake. Most of the court does not have judges or do not report to the court. There is no government bench or no advocate turned up for many cases. I was also told many of them were corrupt. Do you all feel we will get proper judgment? Definitely impossible. This will happen only when stable government is in operation without any once interferences. "

"Let us talk to management for fair deal, else we will go on strike till solution is sought. "

The soldier could understand the situation, left the place and walked towards the village where his troop was stalled. On the way he found many such unrest among those workers could notice some kind of new revolution is on the way. When he reached the place where His camp was situated, found quite isolated without any activities. Many unusual thoughts raised in his mind. He found even their ammunition room was empty. Heavy heart swept his eyes all through and heavy legs tried to reach the place to know whether could get some water out of thrust. Situation seemed serious to know colleagues where about. He found one tent under which saw same boy who was usually roaming about the place earlier for some or other reason. He was seen sitting on some baggage having filled with some grain and eating comfortably some eatable. That sensed him some sort of comfort, and to his lonely soldier sitting behind the tent with big utensil.

Soldier asked him about the grave situation being experienced by him, " Where all our people are? What happened to them?"

"Soldier, I do not worry but how you are here when all went for long march and camping there for a week. There may be some reason behind it but no one knows that. "

By this time soldier was accustomed to such unwarranted events and uncertain situations one has to face. The soldier cook was unaware of his secrete visit for Captain Sinha, hence tried to avoid to answer. He too instead of asking him for any massage from Captain continued to be there at those barracks. For next three days he was moving around various places and market to know the commoners and traders feelings about the ongoing situation. Hardly anyone was interested, except earning money for day to day survival and that was quite natural too. In such situation why so many army, police or some other vehicles were rushing in various places and that confused the soldier. He thought that must be power struggle between the government, army and outsider who were struggling to get the state power in once control. Who were they and what way they want to lead the country? He spent many hours in writing those all details given by French man and the entire motto of the power struggle is under way and the duty of all those peacekeeping force from various nation which were deployed at various places to avoid civil war. While writing he could understand the seriousness and the safety of Humankind.

Captain returned from the camp where they had to fight with those guerrilla who were looting the villagers regularly and even killing in case do not share their money. Their way to collect money was for some political purpose and want to change the system as a whole. They had to camp especially to know the situation on the spot and take the action against who were guilty. Captain thought "this is not enough, but one has to change entirely original thoughts of their misdeeds. But again how to wipe out was real big question to him. We are deputed to control the fights among the community and follow the orders given by top leaders. I know that those many petty and casual robberies and fights are because of poverty and jobless hands. "

Captain wanted to plan the major outbreak in the thoughts of guerrilla and community which was almost in the confused state of mind. Before concluding anything he wanted a feedback from the soldier who was sent to visit the capital city. As soon captain came out of his barrack found soldier was hurriedly coming in search of captain who was already standing just in front. Soldier saluted Captain, but before he speak out the Captain asked him, I was told that you arrived three days back?"

"Yes Captain. " Soldier answered.

"Three days were enough for such work, am I right!"

"Yes you are right. Two days for to and fro travel and two days and half days for search. "

"Collecting some magazine, some books and recent old newspapers were enough should have taken maximum one half day!" Captain was ascertain him.

"It's correct, but I met one French man whose belongs to same place and was working as reporter. He not only had narrated about the place but about political and regional and even historical importance of the Country. Being from India he helped me to gate an accommodation at his friends place. " On hearing that Captain became furious, but controlled his anger till he gets all information. Soldier further informed him all details, which was very important to take further action in case situation gets further detour. "

"It's fine soldier. Give me those books and magazines. " Captain could understood how to approach to such multiple problems.

Soldier stood, instead walking to his place, turned back and said, "Sir, when I arrived I found the boy was roaming about our barracks. He came here to get some food but nothing was available for him. On my question for his arrival here, informed me that a group of some people with rifle arrived. They were searching for ammunition in the strong room. As they could not found anything, left. But carried all the grain and food baggage on their shoulder. Boy followed but vanished in the jungle behind us.

Captain was alerted and gave instruction to the sentries for vigilant for any outsiders who try to invade into our premises. Soon after giving him instructions to the sentry called upon a soldier and instructed him "Now your work is very important to find out those people with rifle were not simple robbers but from gorilla gang. As they fled into jungle behind us likely to attack us and the surrounding places. You will try to find out there where about in jungle. You may take one or 2 smart soldiers along with you. While search operation was taken you have to take optimum precaution keep being separated from each other throughout the search operation. "

The next Day early morning all those three enter the jungle from different places. Every after two hours they will meet at specific point with the help of magnet. They all three walked parallel on the hill top measuring altitude up to 750 yards. They found quiet a good plane land where someone found a trial's hamlets groomed with bamboo trees. They all were in groups, actively busy in some or other and many of them walked down the hill with shovels and axes to carry out for some casual work. It was clear indication to earn money through the work offer they got. Soldier again parted further to get group's dwelling place. While on the way at different places they get those notorious dunked and laying on ground, near their hut. Many were looked busy cooking some meet on wooden fire. All three were taken shelter of large trees trunk and axed tree branches in bunched together. That seemed more than twenty five all together in that group. Soldier decided to go further on search other end of that hill and again the similar scenario was witnessed. It looked most of them taken the shelter of this thicket place and enjoy the life of their liking. It seemed these were the people said to be guerrilla collect money and deposit at the place where that was reached to some political party, But these people were tagged as robbers.

Soldiers reached their barracks with information which was needed by Captain who was busy spreading all newspapers and magazine on the table reading some article published by magazine but his mind was lingered around his soldiers who could be at risk at the hands of those looters. Moreover his curiosity was stronger than his fear, for which he could not remain inside the barrack. As the evening was nearing, he became more worried, unable to concentrate on those right ups, swept aside and was thinking for some other options. He came out of the barrack and went at the hill slop road, saw all soldiers were slowly ascending safely from different direction at a time, amazed him! They all together went into mess where Captain offered them mug of tea. While seeping, Captain asked every one about experience while on their search operation. Experienced one told about those tribe who were busy and did not even cared about my climbing the hill and walking ahead. But he said those were people in group were descending to their work place with all their axe and shovel on their shoulder. Even some lady workers were walking behind them. Some of the men who had been to field work but several of them were strangers on their thick way through bushes came across and struggled to take them away, probably were smugglers. But none of them looking like a tribal. They might not dare to even touch them being part in group. More over those tribe would not involve in such activities of robbery. They are hard worker and know how to earn their daily wedges too! The other soldier said he saw their huts were built in red stone stratum as base and onward with mud and covered by straw all over as roof top. They all seemed together not less than 50 members spread on that plane. The third one who was sure about these being tribe would not harm anyone but there may be some other people who were connected with many atrocious behavior. They never work to earn money but always entangle in some or other such kind of crime. He told Captain " I reached to the place where these criminal were camped in groups at different places had common activities of cleaning rifle, staging and arranging those baggage and loading in some kind of tin trunks. Many of them were idle and drunk while fire was lit outside their huts and some kind of fresh meat was being roasted. "

'Fine soldier. You were rightly narrated, but let me know how you could say they were loading some kind of tin box inside the hut?" Captain asked.

"Sir, afternoon sun rays were the reason made those tin shined and reflected for a while and snapped out. " Soldier informed.

"Good enough soldier. You have clarified my doubts and I am sure they are not ordinary thieveries but those guerrillas who have some connection with some political authority. I will get more idea about their movement till then we must be watchful to protect ourselves and the region for which we are deployed. Now let us work together to help in kitchen for dinner as everything was stolen away, and had to fill needed grocery by this noon. "

Captain was little relaxed for the situation. Those guerrilla wont heart us as their motto was to collect the ammunition in our absence. Their main targets were foreign alliance and business people and large traders. He was certain to those were not helping the state government but some communist who were trying to snatch the power of state. Now whom else were opposing and whom were supporting to be found out? There were three levels- One the state government, second those elected members who were the part of assembly and controlling defense and third outside agencies. We need to find out where commoners support was. Captain, but by this time had begun to understand the meaning of calamity, as if no man's land at present. He hazed in between and the decision makers as whole. Yet he could not stop thinking himself and about anytime civil war would take place.

Morning was pleasant. All soldiers were on ground for their regular exercise. Another scot was were marching in various formation. Third were busy in rehearse, on sharp shooting. Captain walked down around the parade but instantly came back and went to solder's barrack who just returned from city. He entered the room, found scattered scraps of paper laying at the writing desk, and pen for practicing. Some write up.

Captain tried out to get some information but could not get anything. Time did not take care to get lot many information from him, being received many write up through magazines and newspaper. Under the bed neatly written information of his visit clearly stated the overall situation, though casually went through his notes. Captain exclaimed himself, "I regard, it is act of virtue, though I have to get the day to day information from him. " He collected all papers, being few bearings of the places noted in blank and the ends. He sealed them till he speak to him.

When all soldier went to canteen for their brake fast, the favorable wind took him at the sight to explore every acre of its surface in all direction that was not like any adventure but simple walk of the strange land, being near to their barrack. People in market yard know those looked honest creature, would go to any extend for the sake of money. Many times difficult to make out them in the crowd even for those native. Such people go on changing the places of their liking and ceased from troubling themselves. . . While on walk he reached to the twin hill. Delightful walk disturbed by squally sound, thronged his eyes to the direction, stood stand still. The distant sea shore was rare, never to have been seen or near all his life! Time was crucial, the noon brake out had to returned in that sudden bad weather. He turned back, while birds were circulating over his head, was some sign of attack probably on him. But he kept walking till the place was left. On the way he thought that place was good enough for smugglers. He saw some boats moving near the shore and ships were anchor seemed ready for sea. He outlined his intentions so that they do not evaporate like sea mist. He learned when the stakes are high and the pressure is evident, one needs to maintain emotional centeredness and self-control. He was preparing for his future to achieve same thing extra ordinary, which this he understood within himself cutting new grounds and removing old ways only help to achieve what he deiced. Of course with support from locals and if possible, from tribe people from his initiative and risks ahead in his own life. For that he too knows he require extra energy and will power that was also inherited many of those qualities and would work for taking decision with self-controlled attitude.

Soon after lunch he called upon spy soldier in canteen. They both were alone for the free discussion on civilian and political issues in an urban and villagers. Spy soldier was not aware that his some write up were collected from his room under his bed without his knowledge. He was expressionless when captain informed him about his papers lying under the bed. Captain asked about the missing content - and the sentences left half. Spy soldier instead speaking wrote down some words being used by the party as code word. Captain was ascertain the situation like civil war would take place but for that he decided to give training to civilian who were with King holding the state power. Now he had given priority to build roads which were earlier planned by government but put them on hold. He with their consent reorganized the work and employed those local jobless workers. He also started some more construction work like bridges and shelters for poor people. Every one of them were trained to check the sabotages by guerrillas. Apart from soldier's vigilance in and around the region, they tried to collect those tribe from area, knowing their loyalty for the King. Spy soldier once saw the truck full with cotton bales, driven through the same road where road work was carried on. On hearing, Captain asked to follow them with other two soldiers, equipped with guns and allowed them to use in case they open fire on them in self-defense. . . In few hours they returned, with some cotton bales and clothes inside thrown on deck and went out of site in another direction. Captain was sure about their movement, asked other workers to open those bales. The bale was unrolled found silk and cotton bundles, probably for unofficial export. That way the money was exhaled for mutiny. Spy soldier came forward and told Captain about those stolen material from the factory where he saw those workers were on strike and were giving the slogan against the authority, having red flag at the gate. Many such material were lying on ground to show their resentment. He told, he himself witnessed while on his way back. He was also informed on the spot that they even hardly approach to any authority in government or court. The court was only name sake and no matter was resolve without back door money. Most of the time judges were unavailable or no advocate reports. Captain too puzzled, by his explanation. How those bale came out of the factory when people were on strike at gate. Who were those people involved in such two way exploration. For the time being he left the matter as it was and concentrated on the work for which they were deployed. Once again spy and Captain were sitting in canteen, even tea brake hour was over, heard some noise just nearby. Captain searched through the window, could found none. Again same knocking sound appeared. He stood, wide opened the window, saw the boy was sating close to wall below the window, crushing some metallic rounds. Both came out and went near him who was hammering many empty bullets to crush them down. Quarry against the act in the compound of such bullets which were collected by him when some scot of soldiers and some robbers had gun fight. Shell of left over bullets were collected by him to exchange for money. Captain had series of events to resolve and his choice was a long way. Then Soldier produce the visiting card given by French press reporter. Captain was given all the details while visiting those large temples. By this time the soldier was informed about the smuggling of cotton bales and reel of clothes. While on visit of capital city soldier also noticed such bales being transported towards the sea.

This way it was all sure that such theft where to earn illegal money and provide to fulfil political party's motto was very clear to win over the present Democratic Party who is losing its majority in the parliament. Captain thought its seriousness in the matter, decided to visit the French reporter to know detail about internal fight. Though the king of the state is head of parliament but it looked there could be mutiny in future. Captain along with the soldier left for capital by ordinary vehicle and wear common civil dress. Without much efforts they reached to French man who was busy in editing and. arranging some photographs Before entering to his office captain knocked the door while someone from behind walked past pushing him to other side heard, that gentleman's shoes tapping made the French man turn his face toward the door where the knocking along with hard shoes tapping. He saw the tall man with robust personality already entered passed by the earlier door knocked by the stranger. French man looked habitual with such raw and manner less person when the Captain stood behind him waiting for the permission from the French man. Mixed situation raised wrinkle on editors face, stopped that robust man where he was. From distance only asked, "Is it so urgent for you to inform me?"

"Yes Sir. Some of the unknown person were seen on those gate where workers were engaged by some kind of discussions. Possible they wanted to conclude the extended strike. Many of them were joined with their families and children to show their starvation by face and torn cloths. Some leaders were of the opinion to give up the strike instead losing the employment. "

"Now it is too late for them. They should have negotiated earlier with the owner who was in control of his business. " Remarked the Frenchman.

"Sir, there were many unknown who interfered and gave slogans to continue it. "

"O. k. please again go to place and find out how many places such incidents are continued?"

Soon the reporter left the place when Captain was allowed to enter saw the same face of the soldier along with him who was like spy from the peace keeping force. French stood in respect and asked to sit both of them as guest. He made them comfortable by offering Coffee which was already there in the water tight Thermos. Captain who hear the discussion in between reporter and him, said, " Sir, you are already running magazine and also editing those contain to be published but I have suggestion on some of the facts that one should get the information about those striker who are no more loyal with their colleague.

"How do say so? Till date they were regularly sitting in front of the gate and never allowed to transport any finished goods out of premises. " Informed by Frenchman.

"Sir, " Captain took some space before speaking to him, but finally declared, "I think you were under wrong impression about their activities. They were keeping busy everyone at gate but were active behind the factory. They pulled most of the material from stores and transported to the creek by the road just behind military barracks. Since we noticed their movement on regular basis we tried to stop them, but tried to flee away raised our doubts, followed, but thrown some of the cotton bales on the narrow road just below the mountain. After some time we reached to the dead end of the road where the truck was stationed, found empty on our reach. We also checked those launcher waiting there was also without any man inside. We decided to keep night watch to know their movement, found not a single vehicle passed through, but roaring of the truck in the silence hour moved the sentry to rush towards the opposite direction behind the mountain. Soon the truck stationed, systematically everyone rushed to unload which was full with material and shifted to the various launcher waiting to do so. That route was rough but they thought was the safest one, "

"Now, I understand why those owners were stubborn at initial negotiation. I even doubt some people from government itself were also the part of it. It's quite possible they may burn those empty units and pretend that since factory is no more, no more employment is possible. " Disturbed words were spoken by the

Frenchman was true and even Captain added, "They may restart the unit some other places where tribal will be available and no action would be taken against them"

Frenchman concluded, "It's very clear that few people in the power would like to disturb the present set up and society to bring the power of communism"

"Don't you think that would not be fair for those Industrialist who invested their money?"

"No, they would be given enough composition to start another places which they could not do so earlier. " Frenchman explained.

Captain had another challenge to meet when no instruction would be given in such situation. His duty is to inform his immediate controller where situation would go out of control in near future and may ruined many people and establishment and there by employment. Frenchman could understood the crucial stage ahead, looked at Captain who is Indian had great capacity to access the future of country as whole. Frenchman asked his wife to arrange for the lunch, being late afternoon. Captain wanted to visit Ankara before returning to his place but was not allowed to be together at lunch. Wire. Alena who came out in the hall, could recognize the soldier who was with them in last visit. Infect they were with him for his security being new to the place. After their departure, Alena enquire "was that some serious talk was going on, made me away for other work. "

"Do you know who that gentleman was?"

"I could gauge from his face his brilliance, together with his gentle handsome face. "

"You observed him rightly. He is an India Captain who had forecasted the future of this country in such a short period. If we as nationalist should have assessed such conditions earlier before some else do this. Possibly we would not face such rotten life and have better life by this time. "

Captain along with soldier went to see those Hindu Temple all around the city of Ankara, spread over more than 1000 acre land. He saw many of them were already destructed condition by Muslim year. From that period onward many emperor conquered some or other portion of the land and tried to impose their rules at their will. Democratic set up was slowly taken up by different culture of Buddhiazm. Hindu sculpture and their Indian faces were slowly changed over the time. And now there was nothing sure where the Country would lead. Hindu kingdom is still there but without any say in the decision is sad after all. On their returned journey he had many thoughts gathered in his mind. As peace keeping force, he himself did not know to whom support except bringing riots under control. Most of the riots were for food and struggle for authority. Authority was the way to extract money from traders and give to those leaders who were at the facing and watching the changeover. All such incidents reported for money where economy was at stack. It appeared difficult days are ahead where King would be left over alone and possible will be thrown out by communist party where Chinese were already appeared at north east region. That every time he decided to work for those common civilian who were in need of their help from such miscreants. He went to the head of the city in charge and asked them to get those school and hospital work to his people who would complete within the said period. Corporate in charge was aware those corrupted people who would never complete the work unless until get their share. He with the help of sincere officers removed old contractors and handed over rest of the work which was already charted out. One after other work was the only aim would compete within the targeted date. Civilian help was the main reason to achieve the goal win their confidence help to get some sort of stability in the region. That prompted others to follow worked for the while reduced theft and robberies and groups were strictly under watch. Many thousand peace keepers from many other countries were also help to them where Indians were proud to be in leadership and achieved outstanding status being supporting the main system. Captain understood the value support could uplift the moral of the people and understanding among the society would create brother hood spirit which is absent among those people. They unite only when those union leaders were directed by third party who were having different reason, but to disturb and finally make them fight among themselves. Various sites under construction were protected by regional police or national army as were ware of sabotages would take place anytime, as could not stand with the progress. Captain while even on regular work took enough precaution specially bridging the river shores to have quick access to other end while smugglers were active and transporting weapon being sailed through the small boats, and went unchecked. Quite good work apart from supporting the system raise confidence among the people, yet some incident of killing the main contractor disturbed their bridge work. Bridge cement columns were broken before being dried. Captain though approached the authority in concern but did not forget to advice about any large publicity about the incidence that took place. In few days the work was restarted without getting the information the culprit who killed the contractor and damaged the wet cement pillars. Captain anyway did not wanted to hold the work and get delayed the schedule of completion. He had an idea of sending his soldier in civil code as supervisor and workers and work with them. That was how he was able to get day-to-day information about the people working over them. It was so happened once that on completion of that day's work, those people generally go in groups either in nearby market or to their home. The worker sent by captain noticed one of the worker though went with the group up to some distance and diverted himself nearby jungle. He reported the matter to captain about the worker who was not the part of contract worker but someone outsider joined the working group. Next day the supervisor involved in the matter to get the name of that outsider. He could not get that unknown persons in attendance ledger after counting number of people working at the site. Again the supervisor reported this matter to captain while on his round. Captain was clever enough instead asking the name of the person, asked one of the village worker about his where about. But the villager could not get his details who approached his co-worker also answer received was negative created the unknown was from those culprits who damaged the river bridge columns. Captain instead of arresting the unknown culprit reported to police authority to keep a watch on the person who recently regularly coming to work. Captain's advice, not to arrest the culprit by police personal, but to keep the watch on him and follow him and his group activities. Initially we suspected that he was not the same, probably we failed to appreciate the efforts of soldier who disliked him and his work at site. Their staining both existing relationship was hard to understand was the main reason. Moreover mixing with foreign element without reason, was dangerous. This time he was alone not knowing the link between them. I myself misplaced, thought of to take care of him but after consideration not to take risk of taking direct action too, decided to hand over the matter to police. He did not forget to speak about police, who were never disregarded their capabilities but narrated about their great support to achieve most of the project undertaken by the Indian peace keeping force. Last incident where we failed to catch the group who were ware smart enough, fled to unknown place but this time our soldier could trace out their place in the jungle. Head of the state was quite satisfied with captain's work.

Almost four years past for the Indian group in the state of Cambodia was well appreciated, received great applause from the civilians and those regional leaders who were with the king of Cambodia. Captain was aware of his time period is nearing here in Cambodia. Few months were left and now he decided to write all about those work completed and in progress. Now a days he was seen at his desk in the project office on even at his barrack office. That was the day when he was wet by swirly windblown through the barrack where many sheds around were blown off. Except the sentry and the mess staff no one was available. The boy who was on regular visit to the site was found suspicious at the beginning, began helpful in every respect as was also became regular milk supplier and grocery provider to soldier. He reached to Captains office and was additional hand to get collect all those papers and file that was maintained by Captain. He carried safely inside the cell where weapons and ammunitions were stored. Soon after everything was settled down he was taken to canteen where tea was being prepared. Captain suggested whether he would like to join the government job? The boy was happy to hear him who started trusting the unknown orphan boy like him. He obligatory looked at him said, "Sir, I do not feel I will suit their in absences of my education. "

Captain said him support, "You need not worry for your qualification as many places the national cadre required sincere and honest person who can work as national home guard. You will be given training for such job where they were already looking for. " But boy was did not get the confidence on government dut0y which more volatile than his trading and supply work. Initially Captain thought by this time at least regional people would have earned confidence about state authority but unfortunately did not. They were unsure about the democratic system being controlled by various parties and strong hold of communism.

Next day he took some of his juniors along with him to find out the activities on creek sore behind the valley. On the way he could observed the normal movement of trucks busy transporting the goods to shore. He reached to shore to find out the any unofficial goods were transported through the ships were waiting to load before being out from the port. He used his authority to check those documents and country where goods were to be carried out. That was the definite sign of progress and support to present government. He was sure future should be bright provided the same pace of constitutional rules were observed. He also noticed the raw road behind the valley was generally used by smugglers was excavated till the creek shore and always covered by water even at low sea water tide.

Before long sun rays were appeared at barrack, Major Sinha decided to, go to Sea Shore where He sought out so many those smugglers transporting manufactured goods to many other countries, in exchange of money given to them. He also found out money was regularly, donated to those political parties to control the present king and his authorities and the land. But Sinha instead stuck with such situation put his efforts with his efforts to be with city councilor who could manage to help him to rebuild proper roads and block the other end, from where most of the smugglers used those jungle roads. He proposed and allowed to bracket the wall near the Shore. It's now easy for the police and army to have a proper check post near their activities to have close watch. Major and Captain again decided to have a visit towards the capital –Phnom Penh of the land to observe the situation of the strong leaders but, eventually they found king is only for name sake but his followers are leaning towards the communism. They are unable to declare themselves their support to communism as most of the common people in the country are in favor of common parties rule in a democratic war. Possibly the situation being likely be changed provided the common people were regarded their every days need. Presently they were getting plenty of jobs and food to eat because of their engagement in construction and manufacturing activities as many sick companies and factories being started operating at new locations and this kind of work was a blow on such people who are negative against the local authorities and government as whole. The stagnant market was diluted due to mobilization goods and food items mainly the as were strictly exported under authorized agencies. Sinha's bit of initiative and work could augmented the need of the people. He along with his assistant travelled that 85 km. by road by private bus services, which too recently re-operated. They both stepped out some km away to know the real motivation within the citizen. Most of the Industries were demolished being relocated to remote areas to save them from mafia working under different politicians. On the way they also found many courts were under pressure where once no one were turning around. Yet most of those places found those debris laying around those market area and elsewhere. Few meter away they were crossing a long route of wide spread garden. Huge trees were mere attraction to through it but most of those saplings were dried. Very few plants were starving due to lack of water. Most of the places were occupied by stray dogs and animals. Difficult to walk though sheet and cow dunk. Major remarked, "it's the beautiful place located near the lake had many advantages turned into wasteland full by debris all over.

Few hours rest for tiered workers was like heaven for them ruined. It's also sign for those people in charge concentrated to line up lifesaving priories over beautification and entertainment. " Captain realized many other ways but could not hold himself telling to his assistance, '' the world know too little about the extremely harsh experience Cambodia has had with communism. The Khmer Rouge (Red Khmer) regime, led by dictator Pol Pot, killed approximately two million people in the name of communist Ideology. Cambodia now going through process of coming to terms with this un imagible political violence by collecting data and memories and building the future on the basis of solid historical memory. The healing process is just the cause of it where we are here for that. . . "

Soldier who had some knowledge, asked Captain Sinha, '' When Indian culture was well established in Cambodia, how others could spread to other culture?"

"You are right. Those days Buddhism was quickly spread and majority had accepted being also the partly contained culture of Hinduism. Now listen, more changeover was because of the Cambodian Civil War- while in 1967 in urgency had been unplanned, Khmer tried all PNVA/ Viet Cong forces were to with Cambodian civil was to draw from Cambodian soil within 72 hrs. Last minute efforts on the part of U. S. to arrange peace agreement. (Khmer) was a civil war in Cambodia fought between the force of communist party of Kampuchea (known as the Khmer Rouge, supported by North Vietnam and Viet Cong) against the government forces of Kingdom of Cambodia after October 1970, the hammer republic, which had succeeded the kingdom (both supported by U. S and south Vietnam)

The struggle was complicated by the influence and actions of allies of the two Vietnam (PAVAN) involvement was designed sanctuaries in the eastern Cambodia without which it would have been hard to peruse presence was at first tolerated by Prince Shanika, the Cambodian head of the state, but domestic resistance government Kamer Rouge alarm Shinnok and caused him to go to Moscow to request soviet rein in behavior of North Vietnam. The deposition of Sinhala by the Cambodian national assembly in March 1970. Following with wide scale protest in the capital against the presence of PAVN troops in the country, put a pro-American government in power (later declared the Khmer Republic) which demanded that the PAVM leave Cambodia. The Khmer Rouge, promptly invaded Cambodia force. Between March and 1970 the North Eastern third of the country in the engagement with Cambodian army, , the North Vietnamese turned over some of the conquest and provided other assistance to Khmer Rouge, thus empowering what was at the time a small guerilla movement The Cambodian government hastened to expand its army to combat the North

Vietnamese and the growing power of Khmer Rouge. " Captain took a pause for some time, made solider to clarify the main thyme in the editorial written by some experienced writer. He asked him, "In short the U. S. was motivated by the desire to buy time for the withdrawal from Southeast Asia, to protest its ally in South Vietnam and spread of communism to Cambodia. America and South and North Vietnamese forces directly participated in fighting. The U. S. assisted the central government with massive U. S. aerial bombing campaigns and direct material and financial aid, while the North Vietnamese kept soldiers on the lands that they previously occupied and occasionally engaged with the Khmer Republic Army in ground combat. " Captain listened to him carefully and weighed his knowledge. He also shocked to know about him that he was from intelligence and came to review the situation before Captain was too relieved for next assignment in India. Captain was also explained the stock of all affaires he faced during his term. He further farther explained what could be future of that country. "Next five years will be tough for the present Republic government would defeat when victorious Khmer Rouge may proclaim the establishment of Democratic Kampuchea. That time refugee crisis would be on top. Nearly 25% population would be displaced from the rural areas into cities In Pham Pink, it was already grew from 600, 000 in 1970 and would grow further Children were widely used during and after the war and often being persuaded or forced to commit atrocities. More than estimated properties would be destroyed by today and likely to increase further. "All such discussion was under the old banyan tree where those factory workers used to rest at the time of factory strike. From the distance they saw on the large Iron Gate and quite decent house, mostly for visitors. They walked down to the worn out painted house with broken window glass pans and tilted wooden door. From the window it could see many pasted pictures of the garden. Once upon the time, the garden was one of the greatest and beautiful garden in the South Asia. The pictures were about many stalls erected around the garden where containing the various kinds of flower in the cane baskets for sale. The huge crowd where giving quiet a good business to the vendors. It was also wonderful various kinds of water fountain containing some flower petals in and around those water tanks. But today is the entire place became dry and over note. The captain and his assistant felt very sorry for the state of affairs in the past. The captain and his assistant were to step out of the garden where stopped by one of the gentleman, maybe French looked from his attire. He saw both as visitors and asked them, "can I join with you sir. I'm resident of this town. I help visitors and try to explain our culture"

Captain was in word very happy to get someone to explain about the society and the culture of the region.

Captain accepted and shook his hand generously with French man, pointed out at one of the old cement bench under the old tree. French man was very happy at time where someone is ready to listen to him as was searching for someone to whom he could narrate the history.

France was also to be in charge of Cambodia's foreign and trade relations as well as provide military protection. Siam later recognized the protectorate after France ceded the Cambodia province of Battambang and recognize Thai control of Angkor.

France and Cambodia have a special relationship due to shovel history Francophonie and France's role in furthering development in Cambodia.

Cambodia became a French protectorate in 1964 to 1967. It joined Vietnam (Cochin China Annan and Tokin), to form Indochina. Laos added latter. 07th July2005, French explorer arrived in Cambodia in the early 1860's, were seeking to expand French commercial interests in Southeast Asia. In addition to Cambodian Battalion, the Brigade was composed of French Colonial and Vietnamese light Infantry regiments and support element.

23 Jan 2014, - France has largest Cambodian diaspora communities outside the United States, largely because of the refugees who fled there to escape.

Cambodia - France are the bilateral relations between the kingdom Cambodia and France Republic Cambodia was a protectorate of France from 11 Aug.

1863 to 1953. King Norodom approached France in 1861, in attempt to stop neighbors Thailand and Vietnam from swallowing Cambodia land.

A treaty signed in 1863 by King Norodom and approved by his counterpart Norodom III. Cambodia officially became a protectorate of France Empire on 11 Aug. 1863 (1) Cambodia gained independence in November 1953. France and Cambodia enjoy close relations, stemming partly from the days of the France Protectorate and partly from the role played by France Government in signing of the Peace agreement in Paris. in 1991 and further cemented by the France language. These relations are gradually adopted to Cambodians growing integration into its regional environment and its progress towards the status of a middle income country, hopefully by 2020. The "orientation and cooperation Document" signed in 2010, steers our cooperation towards the following goal. 'Support economic growth and job creation in Cambodia by developing human capital and promoting French capital investment. As France was a part of the United Nations Transitional Authority in Cambodia, French President Charles de Gaulle visited Cambodia in 1966 and was given a warm welcome by Norodom Sihanouk.

"I have lived in Phnom Penh for nearly 10 years, and thought that I know the city well. " The gentleman continued his own experience, descended the staircase and opened the door of the flat, a much older model appeared. The apartment had slotted royal -blue shutters and tiled, dusty floor. There were no air conditioner. Ceiling fan pushing hot air around. From the living rooms windows whose many lock stack three minutes to open. Small steps led down a low - slung balcony. Five minutes earlier, we would been immersed in a busting Phnom Penh. There inside, past and present merged. We were being shown an apartment win French colonial roots by a transplanted by a Frenchman 60 years after King Norodom Sihanouk led the crusade for the independence from France in 1953. Perhaps the strongest thing was that there was nothing strange about it.

Despite the sprouting of sky scrapers, the arrival of mega malls, the rise of the English as dominant second language and hurried urban development of commerce has seen an uptick in small to medium enterprises. According to French Embassy, the number of French citizens living in Cambodia has doubled over pass 10 years and grown at an average 10 percent over past three years. French has one of the largest Cambodian diaspora communities outside the United States largely because of the refugees when fled to escape the terror of Khmer Rouge in the 1970's. In recent years, many have been coming here.

In Phnom Pen, I have met a lot of French people without going out of my way to meet French people. Our land lord at that time, we looked at the apartment was

French. A skinny French guy had shown us another apartment weeks before. I ate at French restaurant, bars and cafes every week. Some of them, like the apartment, were in refurbished version of buildings constructed during the French Protectorate, which started in 1863 and ended under Sihanouk 90 years later.

Although the Protectorate way dismantled six decades ago, the French -Cambodian relationship seems to have continued in a less exploitative form, after the watch of the breakup remained friends.

Captain and soldier sat quietly till he was speaking nonstop like history professor in detail. They both too wanted to know the country as such in depth to understand the people and their interest. Many in group with many interest were dividing the society and culture for many reasons but what was hidden in common people was to be seen and worth too. Communist were busy doing all sorts of tactics to brake the unity among those patriotic with the help of military but the Peace Keeping Forces alertness kept them in control knowing fully could relapsed any moment. Captain kept major points in control and now his work for public already began to show the results.

The time to proceed to their barrack before sun sets behind those mountains. Gathered much of the information received from French man was more than enough. In fact he wanted to narrate his own episode when he lodged in one of the good hotel. We asked his contact no. which gave us without any hesitation, though found little nervous to meet him some other occasion. Many three wheelers passed by without notice, helped us to manage one of the loaded vehicle with some plastic roll. That was not the time to be curious to find out in details but to judge ourselves was being carried out to near city where we too were to get down before being walked down. Nearly two hours walk through deem traffic, brought near to barrack. To our surprise silent barrack, surged the wave of some suspicious act, but was alas, found enough sound spread out of canteen, kept the heart cool.

Captain went to his barrack without discussing about the visit, kept winding his luggage for tomorrow where his was to report back to his head quarter in India with little brake for his village on the way. Major took the charge from him with his secret notes and some maps he managed and the civil work in progress. Fair well was the routine which was honored to him. While on the beginning of way many people from the periphery could found him out because of his services, waved at him, and was also sentimental moment where he was never to see them again in his life.

Two days intermittent travel made him tired. He boarded the train for his village, had no information there and late evening his walk through semi tar road was lingering with many mixed memories he had, reached near village where one old temple on the bank of small rivulet. Some old aged person there could notice him but could not make him out. His surprised come home, made every one there chirp and thronged around him, emotionally cooled down after embracing. . Father noticed his tiredness, requested every one there not to inform villagers till other day.

Next day early morning without any information, he went to the field where his project was carried out. To his surprise, even in the summer he could notice thick green crop standing in field, surrounded by many other plantation in its support. Novel idea he never though off. He tempted to reach to those large abandon, challenging orphaned land. While going through he saw the tractor which was used kept aside for overhauling made him quite happy for the interest youngster kept going. He saw someone was bringing some spare parts of it, left it half way to meet Captain. No way but had to wait for him, took his hands, while tears rolled down. Instead share of any information, both walked down to the fields, which was far away. He too was in hurry to have a lot, but even from distance could make out the length of paddy green crop spread over. He could not believe nearly 50 acre odd baron was turned into greenery. "Great Work" He put his hand on the fellow, though was till now unknown to him. Many from nearby village mostly were new once surrounded to Captain. Everyone there wanted to share some or other experience about the work they carried out and how such large abandon land was received from Tehsil. He was shocked to hear them though no one was present from his initial project. Being unaware of his unaccepted visit here. He asked them why this permanent construction is going on. "This for grain storages. Quit good amount of paddy crop is expected, and this is common to all and would be distributed equally who put their efforts. "

"Good enough, Keep it on" Captain had no words to speak but could hold his emotions. Looked at all those standing around and their feelings how out of his small guidance~ could make out such wonderful results. While returning home many more joined through were stopped by two army officers, seems newly appointed by their over enthusiastic approach, stood in line by giving strong salute to Captain there on the field. Spoke in loud voice - " Jay Jawan Jay Kisan. " Captain moved by this sudden high spirited emotional attack where all others too followed the slogan to repeat. All their stood for a while in silence to pray for those who led their life for the Nation which was just won and lost after all. Those two were selected from the very group he trained and also were too are followed by many others.

He was to be there with all villagers to share many sensible incidents occurred and solved on the way. His casual leave for a week was kept for them, but all of sudden he got a warrant to reach to the head quarter immediately and that was left every one unaware and was known to them only early morning when he was already in train for his destination. People in the village gauzed many way as they though as indusial, but parents had no answer for it. But father conveyed his message while departing, said "keep the slogan alive by all efforts".

Villagers had novel idea to keep the slogan alive painted some boards and grouted at the entrance and many other places.

Many weeks passed on reply from the captain or even from his head quarter where he was to report. Whenever father wrote them, the answer was only in one line – "secret mission" Many months passed Father being ex-service man could gauze something is very serious and would be difficult to his where about. What could be was always question to him was making him mentally sick and was almost on bed till his death. Even that tragic incident too never helped his son to return for the cause. Time lagged behind and people of the village had no other go but to remember him and share many memories about him specially, when many other selected candidate were on pre village leave.

One day night many army people arrived with his body covered with National Flag followed by many social workers. Entire village gone had no strength to bear the shock, gone in silence. New visitors kept on gauzing those villagers faces in grief and the slogan of – Jay Jawan, Jay Kissan – underneath –By Lal Bahadur Shastriji. And Captain Sinha.

Many artist throng to make his statue at free of cost but villagers were reluctant to get such offer with reimbursing at least at actual cost. Yet many made his sculpture of their own.

One may get similar story having such many factual incidents. But as Author of this book I would give my suggestions for all those army/ defense personal to use their laser time while working or even after retirement for such activities where most of them belongs to village and have great advantage over others. Many agriculture graduate at initial stages work in some government or corporate sector but leave those comfortable services and try to utilize their knowledge to develop their own land and earn much more than even their expectation. I love villagers for their work and straight forward nature which valued in India. God Bless Them All. Farmers are real strength of the Nation and India is the one

Where its main occupation is farming. Unfortunately realized by Government very late.

THE STORY IS TO BE CONTINUED FURTHER MAY BE IN SOME OTHER FORM. ~

www.ingramcontent.com/pod-product-compliance
Lightning Source LLC
LaVergne TN
LVHW061553070526
838199LV00077B/7031